AN OXFORD

Cover and frontispiece: The Radcliffe Camera.

PEDLAR'S PACK   4

AN OXFORD ASSORTMENT

Collected and presented
by
SOPHIE BLACKSELL

Illustrations by John Searl

EX LIBRIS PRESS

Published in 1997 by
EX LIBRIS PRESS
1 The Shambles
Bradford on Avon
Wiltshire
BA15 1JS

Design and typesetting by
Ex Libris Press

Cover printed by Shires Press, Trowbridge
Printed and bound by Cromwell Press, Melksham

ISBN 0 948578 82 3

A note on the illustrations:
Cover and frontispiece: The Radcliffe
Camera; page 8: Magdalen College;
page 30: A Prospect of Dreaming Spires;
page 44: Christ Church; page 66: Inside
the Bodleian; page 76: Gargoyle, New
College; page 90: Bridge of Sighs linking
Hertford College across New College
Lane; page 108: Rhodes House.

Contents ~

ରଧ   Oxford owes its name and existence to a cattle-crossing over the River Thames.

ରଧ   The Saxon settlement which grew up between the Thames and the Cherwell was fortified by the Normans. A castle was built on the west side of the city to defend it against Danish invaders.

ରଧ   Before the end of the twelfth century, Oxford (already a thriving religious centre) had also established itself as a place of scholarship and learning. St. Mary's Church in the High Street was the centre of the medieval University.

ରଧ   In the thirteenth century the first colleges were founded. Balliol, Merton and University Colleges qualify as the oldest in the University.

ରଧ   Oxford University emerged dominant from the Middle Ages, using its privileges to assert its supremacy over the city. For centuries, the Chancellor of the University had almost exclusive authority in matters of law and order in the city.

ଔ   During the Civil War, Oxford became a Royalist stronghold. King Charles I held court at Christ Church, and the Queen resided at Merton.

ଔ   Eighteenth century Oxford was renowned for decadence, drinking and 'dandies'.

ଔ   At the beginning of the twentieth century, William Morris, later to become Lord Nuffield, began a bicycle business in Oxford, which quickly developed into the world famous Morris Motors. The car factory at Cowley has provided Oxford with another focus of employment and interest; a rival to the University which had dominated the city for so long.

ଔ   Famous throughout the world and visited by hoards of visitors each year, Oxford today is involved in a sophisticated balancing act: not only, as throughout her history, must she maintain her equilibrium in the interplay of Town and Gown, but also counterpoise the requirements of twentieth century urban life with the claims of her rich and irrepressible past.

Sophie Blacksell
Oxford, December 1996

Oxford from the Sublime to the Ridiculous

Oxford must be one of the most literary cities in Great Britain. Not only has it produced some great writers of its own from among the many young hopefuls who join the ranks of its University each year, but it has also inspired the apparently casual visitor to try and capture the unique atmosphere of the place in poetry and prose. Facing such a mountain of textual effusions, I may well join with the eighteenth century poet Thomas Tickell when he exclaims:

> Where shall I first the beauteous scene disclose,
> And all the gay Variety expose?
> For wheresoe'er I turn my wond'ring Eyes,
> Aspiring Tow'rs, and verdant Groves arise,
> Immortal Greens the smiling Plains array,
> And mazy Rivers murmur all the way.

Perhaps in such a case it would be best to start with some descriptions of the city's situation in verse and prose from a varied assortment of visitors and inhabitants. Let us begin in the sixteenth century with Ralph Aga's Map of Oxford:

> The measure form and sight I bring
> Of ancient Oxford, nobleness of skill
> A city seated rich in everything,
> Girt with woods and water, pasture, corn and hill:
> He took the vewe from north, and so he leaves it still,
> For there the buildings make the bravest show,
> And from those walks the scholars best it know.

છ

One hundred years later a single woman, the intrepid Celia Fiennes, riding side-saddle through England, recorded her first impressions of the city:

Oxford opens to view 2 mile off, its scituation is fine on a round hill, environ'd round with hills adorn'd with Woods and Enclosures, yet not so neare as to annoy the town, which stands pleasant and compact; there is a fine Causy for near two mile by the road for the schollars to walke on; the Theater stands the highest of all and much in the middle encompass'd with the severall Colledges and Churches and other Buildings whose towers and spires appeares very well at a distance; the Streetes are very cleane and well pitched, and pretty broad, the High Streete is a very noble one, soe large and of a great length; in this is the university Church, called St. Maryes, which is very large and lofty but nothing very Curious in it.

☙

And here is Daniel Defoe, at the beginning of the eighteenth century, describing his visit to Oxford in his Tour through the Whole Island of Great Britain:

From hence I came to *Oxford*, a Name known throughout the Learned World; a City famous in our *English* History for several Things, besides its being an University.

1. So Eminent for the goodness of its Air, and Healthy Situation; that our Courts have no less than three Times, if my Information is right, retir'd hither, when *London* has been visited with the Pestilence; and here they have been always safe.

2. It has also several Times been the Retreat of our Princes, when the rest of the Kingdom has been embroil'd in War and Rebellion; and here they have found both Safety and Support; at least, as long as the Loyal Inhabitants were able to protect them.

3. It was famous for the noble Defence of Religion, which our first Reformers and Martyrs made here, in their Learned and bold Disputations against the Papists, in behalf of the

Protestant Religion; and their triumphant closing the Debates, by laying down their Lives for the Truths which they asserted.

4.   It was likewise famous for resisting the Attacks of Arbitrary Power, in the Affair of *Magdalen* College, in King *James*'s time; and the Fellows laying down their Fortunes, tho' not their Lives, in Defence of *Liberty* and *Property*.

This, to use a Scripture Elegance, *is that City of* Oxford; the greatest, (if not the most Ancient) University in this Island of *Great-Britain*; and perhaps the most Flourishing at this Time, in Men of Polite Learning, and in the most Accomplish'd Matters, in all Sciences, and in all the Parts of acquir'd Knowledge in the World.

ೞ

At the beginning of our own century, Oxford still conveyed a regal grandeur whatever the weather or the season:

She stands between the hills in a stream-pierced valley; and in that long valley the meadow-land is a little richer, the grass is a little greener and the buttercups and the kingcups are fairer and more golden than in other valleys. Often the mists rise to wrap her closely in their grey swathing, that she may shine more gladly in the dancing sunshine. If thick clouds skulk across the sun, the wind blows with keen anger. On the days when the rain drenches continuously, sullenly down, her beauty ennobles the general distress.

You should see her on a windy morning in the Spring. The young green is leaping to life in the black trees and bare creepers … The sun gleams dazzling out … The great trees have their branches, and the joy of the wind trembles in the bud-laden twigs and sets the creepers quivering with glee against the grey old walls to which their suckers cling. The big river flows by with enormous gaiety stretching itself out to reflect in its broad water as much of the universal joy as it may; the little river overflows its banks, most naughtily in its effort to come nearer to the lady-city, and passes under Magdalen Bridge, softly chuckling to be at last so near her.

You should see her on a still evening in the autumn. The sun is slowly sinking … Quiet broods between heaven and earth – the hush of awe at a ceremony. There is no leaf on any tree which stirs, and all the leaves of the creepers glow tranquilly with colour, as though stayed for that majestic moment in their life's growth up the old walls...The river flows by so silently, it takes the colour of the sky so deeply, that it does not seem to move, but to lie firm and still, like an ancient shield of burnished gold. There is no movement. All things stand at gaze in adoration; only round the turrets and round the tall spires and the pinnacles light trembles and plays in a haze of tremulous colour. Royally the lady-city plays her part in the festival that such an evening is, a festival in honour of the worth and beauty of Life.

Hugh de Selincourt: *Oxford from Within*

 og

One of Oxford's most distinctive personalities, the seventeenth century antiquarian and chronicler Anthony Wood is full of praise for Oxford's position and his measured prose soon overflows into a flood of enthusiastic description:

In the building and planting of the city of Oxon our ancestours and praedicessours have behaved themselves verie wisely and politickly; especially for these respects following. As:

That they have selected a gravelly soile for its station, which by the generality is thought meet and fit; for in such places the air is most commonly cleer sharp and tenuous and not subject to foggs and mists as fat and clayish ground is ...

That they have selected a place where is a sweet wholsome and well-tempered aire, such an air that hath bin publickly admired and applauded by persons far and neare, and soe inticing that it caused the Graeklaudians (as 'tis reported) to change their seat and to settle here that they might plant a scoole of learning.

The hills which are on the south and west part and partly on the north-east side; what greater ornaments can there be for her scituation! Forasmuch as they have and are still partly loyned with woods. The plaines which are on the east and south-east and north part; what more commendable! When at the welcome season of the year they are gloriously mantelled with a delightful verdure, and the winding rivulets which are therein seem from the hills above to the prying spectatour as soe many snakes sporting themselves therein. These are the incomparable conveniences of nature and art that have inticed kings, queens and princes to retire here for refreshment and diversion, and to have built them pallaces both in and neare it. These (with the University) are those inducements that have drawne the representatives of the nation here in severall ages. And such also are the delights that invite forreigners from a farr to receive the benefit of them.

ᘓ

Centuries of writers have been alive to the delights of Oxford's situation and it is often from a distance that Oxford begins to cast her spell:

Upon a hill I stood, and far below
Lay the loved city in a silver haze:
Mine eyes were quick with tears: she lay so fair,
So passionless, so sad.
                    'Twas here our fathers
Drained the waste fen, and with prophetic eyes
Divined a refuge for the soul, and planned
A green oasis severed from the waste,
Where each, in cloistered calm and leisured shade,
Might learn of wisdom in the lap of peace.
Slowly she grew in unobtrusive grace
Generous in bounty as in beauty first:

As showers, as showers of scarlet leaves in autumn,
The generations scatter: she remains
Like Niobe, surviving all her sons:
Shield me, O Mother! For even while I gaze,
I feel the arrow of Apollo's fire.

Gascoigne Mackie: 'Oxford'

ଔ

*Most evocative of all perhaps, are the famous lines by
Matthew Arnold in his poem, 'Thyrsis':*

This winter eve is warm,
Humid the air! leafless, yet soft as spring,
The tender purple spray on copse and briers!
And that sweet city with her dreaming spires,
She needs not June for beauty's heightening.

Lovely all times she lies, lovely tonight!

ଔ

*Despite the traffic difficulties of trying to enter Oxford
nowadays, Arnold's 'dreaming spires' still suggest an
irresistible beauty; history-filled yet timeless, that has fired
the imaginations and emotions of generations of visitors to
the city. In Thomas Hardy's novel,* Jude the Obscure, *the hero
focuses his hopes and aspirations on the distant city as he
views it in the setting sun. Hardy may coyly rename his city,
'Christminster' but it is Oxford, 'unquestionably.'*

Some way within the limits of the stretch of landscape, points of light like the topaz gleamed. The air increased in transparency with the lapse of minutes, till the topaz points showed themselves to be the vanes, windows, wet roof slates, and other shining spots upon the spires, domes, freestone-work, and varied outlines that were faintly revealed. It was Christminster, unquestionably; either directly seen, or miraged in the peculiar atmosphere.

The spectator gazed on and on till the windows and vanes lost their shine, going out almost suddenly like extinguished candles. The vague city became veiled in mist. Turning to the west, he saw that the sun had disappeared. The foreground of the scene had grown funereally dark, and near objects put on the hues and shapes of chimeras.

 og

As one draws closer to Oxford, Jude's 'city of light' takes on substance and the 'dreaming spires' prove to be attached to solid ancient buildings.

The first view of the City of Colleges is always one that will be long remembered. Even the railway traveller, who enters by the least imposing approach, and can scarcely see that he is in Oxford before he has reached Folly Bridge, must yet regard the City with mingled feelings of delight and surprise as he looks across the Christ Church Meadows and rolls past Tom Tower. But he who approaches Oxford from the Henley Road, and looks upon that unsurpassed prospect from

Magdalen Bridge, – or he who enters the city, as Mr Green did, from the Woodstock Road, and rolls down the shady avenue of St. Giles', between St. John's College and the Taylor Buildings, and passes the graceful Martyrs' Memorial, will receive impressions such as probably no other city in the world could convey.

The above extract is taken from The Adventures of Mr Verdant Green, *one of the most famous and popular of the Victorian 'Oxford' novels. Written by the Rev. Edward Bradley, using the pseudonym Cuthbert Bede, the novel traces the university career of its amenable but luckless hero and successfully recreates the atmosphere and foibles of mid-nineteenth century Oxford.*

୯୫

Whether arriving in Oxford as a tourist or a 'fresher', most first-time visitors share Bradley's enthusiasm for the city. In the following extracts two famous sons of the University express their first impressions of Oxford in letters home. First C.S. Lewis to his father:

This place has surpassed my wildest dreams; I never saw anything so beautiful, especially on these frosty nights; though in the Hall of Oriel where we do our papers it is fearfully cold at about four o'clock on these afternoons. We have most of us tried, with varying success, to write in our gloves…

and brother:

Oxford is absolutely topping, and I am awfully bucked with it …

And John Keats, a century before:

12th Sept. 1817

This Oxford I have no doubt is the finest city in the World – it is full of old Gothic buildings – Spires – towers – Quadrangles – Cloisters Groves &c and is surrounded with more clear streams than I ever saw together. I take a walk by the Side of one of them every Evening and thank God, we have not had a drop of rain these many days.

Later on that month, Keats summed up his view of Oxford's appearance in verse:

> The Gothic looks solemn
> The plain Doric column
> Supports an old Bishop and Crosier;
> The mouldering arch
> Shaded o'er by a larch
> Stands next door to Wilson the Hosier.
> Vice – that is, by turns,
> O'er pale faces mourns
> The black tasselled trencher and common hat.
> The chantry boy sings,

The steeple-bell rings,
And as for the Chancellor – dominat.

There are plenty of trees,
And plenty of ease,
And plenty of fat deer for Parsons;
And when it is venison,
Short is the benison, –
Then each on a leg or thigh fastens.

ᘓ

And in his own unmistakeable style, Gerard Manley Hopkins evoked the medievalism that endures in Oxford:

Towery city and branchy between towers;
Cuckoo-echoing, bee-swarmèd, lark-charmèd,
                              rook-racked, river-rounded;
The dapple-eared lily below thee; that country and town did
Once encounter in, here coped and poised powers;

Thou hast a base and brickish skirt there, sours
That neighbour-nature thy grey beauty is grounded
Best in; graceless growth, thou hast confounded
Rural rural keeping – folk, flocks and flowers.
Yet ah! this air I gather and I release
He lived on; these weeds and waters, these walls are what
He haunted who of all men most sways my spirits to peace;

Of realty the rarest-veinèd unraveller; a not
Rivalled insight, be rival Italy or Greece;
Who fired France for Mary without spot.

ದ

*Oxford has also been the subject of some less accomplished
but more effusive verse over the centuries. By liberally
sprinkling their poems with classical analogies and capital
letters, writers sought to convey their reverence for the city.*

Oxford, the Goddess Muse's Native home,
Inspir'd like Athens, and adorn'd like Rome!
Hads't thou, of old been Learnings fam'd Retreat,
And Pagan Muses chose thy lovely Seat,
O, how unbounded had their fiction been!
What fancy'd Visions had adorn'd the Scene!

Thomas Tickell

Ye fretted pinnacles, ye fanes sublime,
Ye towers that wear the mossy vest of time;
Ye massy piles of old munificence,
At once the pride of learning and defence;
Ye cloisters pale that, lengthening to the sight,
To contemplation, step by step, invite;
Ye high-arched walks, where oft the whispers clear
Of harps unseen have swept the poets ear;
Ye temples dim, where pious duty pays
Her holy hymns of ever-echoing praise;

Lo! your lov'd Isis, from the bordering vale,
With all a mother's fondness bids you hail!
Hail, Oxford, hail! of all that's good and great,
Of all that's fair, the guardian and the seat;
Nurse of each brave pursuit, each generous aim
By truth exalted to the throne of fame!
Like Greece in science and in liberty,
As Athens learn'd, as Laecedaemon free.

Thomas Warton: 'Triumph of Isis'

cs

Other visitors have, however, been less than rapturous about the city. When the American Nathaniel Hawthorne (a nineteenth century Bill Bryson) visited briefly in 1856 he was supremely unimpressed:

Oxford is an ugly old town, of crooked and irregular streets; gabled houses, mostly plastered of a buff or yellow hue; some new fronts, and as for the buildings of the University, they seem to be scattered at random without any reference among one another. I passed through the old gateway of Christ Church, and looked at its enclosed square; and that is, in truth, pretty much all I have seen of the University of Oxford. From Christ Church, we rambled along a street that led us to a bridge across the Isis; and we saw many row-boats lying in the river – the lightest craft imaginable, unless it were an Indian canoe. The Isis is but a narrow stream, and with a sluggish current. I believe the students of Oxford are famous for their skill in rowing.

Hawthorne did however change his mind about Oxford during a longer stay a few months later:

If I remember aright, I spoke very slightingly of the exterior aspect of Oxford, as I saw it with Julian, during an hour or two's stop here, on my way to Southampton. I am bound to say, that my impressions are now very different, and that I find Oxford exceedingly picturesque, and rich in beauty and grandeur and antique stateliness. I do not remember very particularly what we saw; gray weather-stained, and picturesquely time-worn fronts of famous colleges and halls of learning, everywhere about the streets, with arched entrances, passing through which, we found grassy quadrangles within, with perhaps a cloistered walk around; old gray towers and turrets, ivy grown; quaint bits of sculpture from monkish hands, the most grotesque and ludicrous faces, as if the slightest whim of these old carvers took shape in stone, the material being so soft and manageable by them; an ancient stone pulpit in the quadrangle of Maudlin College, one of only three now extant in England; a splendid – or not splendid, but dimly magnificent chapel belonging to the same college, with painted windows, of rare beauty, not brilliant with diversified hues, but of a sombre tint. In this Chapel, there is an alabaster monument – a recumbent figure of the founder's father, as large as life – which, though several centuries old, is as well preserved as if fresh from the chisel. But I cannot separate these things in my recollection; they are all jumbled together, pretty much as if the antiquities of Oxford were tossed together into one heap of gray stones.

Hawthorne's confusion is typical of anyone sightseeing in Oxford. There are so many things to see: so many colleges, churches, monuments all built in the same mellow stone from the local quarries, and so many names to remember: famous architects and academics, royal visitors and future prime ministers, and so much has happened there that … Poor Mr Green Senior quite understandably finds his guided tour of the sights more than a little muddling.

The short, thick stick of the guide served to direct attention to the various objects he enumerated in his rapid career. "This here's Christ Church College," he said, as he trotted them down St. Aldate's, "built by Card'nal Hoolsy four underd feet long and the famous Tom Tower as tolls wun underd and wun hevery night that being the number of stoodents on the foundation;" and thus the guide went on, perfectly independent of the artificial trammels of punctuation, and not particular whether his hearers understood him or not: that was not his business. And as it was that gentleman's boast that he "could do the alls, collidges, and principle hedifices ina nour and a naff," it could not be expected but that Mr Green should take back to Warwickshire otherwise than a slightly confused impression of Oxford. When he unrolled that rich panorama before his 'mind's eye,' all its component parts were strangely out of place …

But if such a shrewd and practised observer as Sir Walter Scott after a week's hard and systematic sight-seeing, could only say of Oxford, "The time has been too short to convey to me separate and distinct ideas of all the variety of wonders that I saw: my memory only at present furnishes a grand but indistinct picture of towers, and chapels, and oriels, and vaulted halls, and libraries, and paintings;" – if Sir Walter Scott could say this after a week's work, it is not to be wondered at that Mr. Green, after so brief and rapid a survey of the city, at the heels of an unintelligent guide, should feel himself slightly confused when on his return to the Manor Green, he attempted to give a slight description of the wonderful sights of Oxford.

(The Adventures of Mr Verdant Green)

ↂ

And if this is what a tour was like in the Victorian era, the progress of the twentieth century does not seem to have improved matters much:

TOURISTS' ROUND

Marcato con brio
> Into the Chapel and round the Quad,
> Up the Turl and down the Broad,
> Through the Kitchen and up the Stair,
> Hurry on, madam; quicker, sir.

Presto
> Here's the glove Elizabeth wore.
> Mark the genuine Norman door.

This is Cardinal Wolsey's hat,
And that is where the Parliament sat.

Rallentando
        (I could do with a seat – and how!
        Not now, darling, hush, not now!)
Prestissimo
        Keble's the one that's made of brick.
        Magdalen's strong on the perpendic.
        Gilbert Scott on the left, and then
        On the right for Christopher Wren.
        Notice the Epstein on your way,
        Very symbolical, so they say.

Rallentando
        (I think - you know – I'm feeling queer.

Dolorosamente
        What I need is a glass of beer.
        Hush dear,
        Not beer,
        Not here.)

Marcato
da capo.
        Into the Chapel and round the Quad
        Up the Turl …

 C3

Perhaps on the whole it is better for first-time visitors to walk around Oxford alone to discover for themselves the atmosphere of the place. This is what Jude does when he finally reaches his dreamed-for 'Christminster':

It was a windy, whispering, moonless night. To guide himself he opened under a lamp a map he had brought. The breeze ruffled and fluttered it, but he could see enough to decide on the direction he should take to reach the heart of the place.

After many turnings he came up to the first ancient mediaeval pile that he had encountered. It was a college as he could see by the gateway. He entered it, walked around, and penetrated to dark corners that no lamplight reached. Close to this college was another; and a little further on another; and then he began to be encircled as it were with the the breath and sentiment of the venerable city. When he passed objects out of harmony with its general expression he allowed his eyes to slip over them as if he did not see them.

A bell began clanging, and he listened till a hundred-and-one strokes had sounded. He must have made a mistake, he thought: it was meant for a hundred.

When the gates were shut, and he could no longer get into the quadrangles, he rambled under the walls and doorways, feeling with his fingers the contours of their mouldings and carving. The minutes passed, fewer and fewer people were visible, and still he serpentined among the shadows, for had he not imagined these scenes through ten bygone years, and what was a night's rest for once? High against the black sky the flash of a lamp would show crocketed pinnacles and indented battlements. Down obscure alleys, apparently never trodden now by the foot of man, and whose very existence seemed to be forgotten, there would jut into the path porticoes, oriels, doorways of enriched and florid middle-age design, their extinct air being accentuated by the rottenness of the stones. It seemed impossible that modern thought could house itself in such decrepit and superseded chambers.

൵

A decade after Hardy's tragic tale of unfulfilled aspiration and social alienation, Oona Howard Ball published Barbara Goes to Oxford, *a semi-autobiographical account of an Edwardian lady's first trip to Oxford. Barbara's experiences are far less harrowing than Jude's, consisting chiefly of sight-seeing and social calls, but she too makes an initial tour of the city, following the route of the old city walls.*

After tea we set forth. We looked out our way before we went, for who does not despise the obvious tourist who consults his map in the street? We slipped our little guide-book into our pocket in case of real need.

We started along a street made fragrant by the scent of many lime-trees; the wall of St. John's College on our right, on our left the garden of the Warden of Wadham.

We turned down Holywell Street, which is narrow and winding and full of ancient houses. Some of these had just been pulled down, and, through the gaps, one caught glimpses of the old city wall which is still standing here. Then into Longwall Street, delightfully and descriptively named, and so into the High Street. The sun was setting behind St. Mary's Church and the beautiful curving street was a path of glory. I was reluctant to turn away from it, but Brownie was inexorable …

So we turned down Rose Lane and went into Christ Church meadows, under the bastions of the old walls and out by the Water Gate into St Aldate's (which is pronounced St. Old's). Then along Brewer Street, narrow and dark, and so into Paradise Square …

We went up Castle Street and along New Inn Hall Street, and so out into the Cornmarket just where the North Gate used to stand. The Norman tower of St. Michael's rose cold and grey against a sky of chrysopase green … Slowly we went along Broad street, past the Sheldonian theatre, and so home.

We have walked all around our new domain, our fairy city. We feel as though we have drawn a cordon of love and reverence about it, and so have made it ours for evermore. We sat for a long time at our window … The only sounds we heard were the hooting of the owls and the gentle rustling of one tall poplar in the breeze.

Here we hushed and blessed ourselves with silence for a space and then went off to bed.

Oxford on Isis

John Keats apparently spent his first weeks at Oxford on the river:

For these last five or six days, we have had regularly a boat on the Isis, and explored all the Streams about, which are more in number than your eyelashes. We sometimes skim into a bed of rushes, and there become naturalised riverfolks – there is one particularly nice nest which we have christened 'Reynold's Cove', in which we have read Wordsworth and talked as maybe.

The rivers have always played an important part in Oxford life. The reason for the original settlement, they now form the focus for some unique Oxford pastimes. The main river is the Thames, although in typical Oxford fashion it is given the more romantic name of Isis as it passes through the city:

The famous River Isis hath her spring
Neare Tetbury and downe along doth bring
(As hand-maids) to attend her progress, Churne,
Colne, Windrush, Yenload, Leech, whose windings turne
And Meads and Pastures trims, bedecks and dresses,
Like an unvaluable chaine of Esses.
After release of many a Ducke and Goose,
At Saint John's Bridge they make their rendevous,
And there like robbers crossing London way,
Bid many a barefoot Welshman wade or stay,
Close under Oxford, one of England's eyes,
Chief of the chiefest Universities.
From Banbury, desirous to add knowledge
To zeal and to be taught in Magdalen College,
The River Cherwell doth to Isis runne
And bears her company to Abingdon.

John Taylor, 'The Water-Poet', 1632

൚

*The Isis also makes an appearance in Edmund Spenser's epic
poem, 'The Faerie Queene' as the bridegroom's mother at
the marriage of the Thames and the Medway:*

The Ouze, whom men doe Isis rightly name;
Full weake and crooked creature seemed shee,
And almost blind through eld, that scarce her way could see…

Therefore on either side she was sustained
Of two small grooms, which by their names were hight
The Churne and the Charwell, two small streames, which pained
Themselves her footing to direct aright,
Which fayled oft through faint and feeble plight:
But Thame was stronger, and of better stay;
Yet seem'd full aged by his outward sight,
With head all hoary, and his beard all gray,
Deawed with silver drops, that trickled downe alway.

And eke he seemed to stoupe afore
With bowed backe, by reason of the lode,
And that heavy burden, which he bore
Of that faire city, wherein make abode
So many learned impes, that shoote abrode,
And with their branches spread all Britany,
No lesse then do her elder sisters broode.
Joy to you both, ye double noursery,
Of Arts, but Oxford thine doth Thame most glorify.

∞

It is on the Isis, below Christchurch meadows, that the College boat races take place in February and May. Because the river is very narrow at some points, the boats line up one behind the other instead of starting side by side; the object of the exercise being to 'bump' the boat in front. A 'Bumps' race is fast, frenzied and often chaotic.

Tom Brown, who famously epitomised the ideal of the honest and plucky public school-boy, continues his gentlemanly career at St. Ambrose College, Oxford in Tom Brown at Oxford. *Tom, of course, takes to rowing, that most hearty of sports, like the proverbial duck to water. The extract that follows, evokes the tension and exhilaration of Tom's first Oxford boat race, creating an atmosphere that generations of student rowers will recognise.*

There it comes at last – the flash of the starting gun … The starting ropes drop from the coxswain's hands, the oars flash into the water, and gleam on the feather, the spray flies from them, and the boats leap forward.

The crowds on the banks scatter, and rush along, each keeping as near as may be to its own boat. Some of the men on the towing-path, some on the very edge of, often in, the water; some slightly in advance, as if they could help to drag their boat forward; some behind, where they can see the pulling better; but all at full speed, in wild excitement, and shouting at the top of their voices to those on whom the honour of the college is laid.

"Well pulled all!" "Pick her up there, five!" "You're gaining every stroke!" "Time in the bows!" "Bravo St. Ambrose!"

On they rush by the side of the boats, jostling one another, stumbling, struggling and panting along.

For a quarter of a mile along the bank the glorious, maddening hurly-burly extends, and rolls up the side of the stream…

The two crowds are mingled now, and no mistake; and the shouts come all in a heap over the water … The water rushes by, still eddying from the strokes of the boat ahead. Tom fancies now he can hear their oars and the workings of their rudder, and the voice of the coxswain.

In another moment both boats are in the Gut, and a perfect storm of shouts reaches them from the crowd as it rushes madly off to the left to the footbridge, amidst which "Oh well steered, well steered, St. Ambrose!" is the prevailing cry. Then Miller, motionless as a statue till now, lifts his right hand and whirls the tassel round his head. "Give it her now, boys; six strokes and we're into them." Old Jervis lays down that great broad back, and lashes his oar through the water with the might of a giant, the crew catch him up in another stroke, the tight new boat answers to the spurt, and Tom feels a little shock behind him, and then a grating sound, as Miller shouts, "Unship oars, bow and three! " and the nose of the St. Ambrose boat glides quietly up to the side of the Exeter, till it touches their stroke oar.

૬૩

Verdant Green's attempts at rowing are somewhat less successful:

He had left the Christ Church meadows far behind, and was beginning to feel slightly exhausted by his unwonted exertions, when he reached that bewildering part of the river termed 'the Gut'. So confusing were the intestine commotions of this gut, that, after passing a chequered existence as an aquatic shuttlecock, and being assailed with a slang-dictionary-full of opprobrious epithets, Mr. Verdant Green caught another tremendous crab, and before he could recover himself, the 'tub' received a shock, and, with a loud cry of "Boat ahead!" ringing in his ears, the University Eight passed over the place where he and "the Sylph" had so lately disported themselves.

With the wind nearly knocked out of his body by the blade of the bow-oar striking him on the chest as he rose to the surface, our unfortunate hero was immediately dragged from the water … "not dead but very wet!" and forthwith placed in safety in his deliverers boat. .

This little adventure (for a time at least) checked Mr Verdant Green's aspirations to distinguish himself on the river; and he therefore renounced the sweets of the Isis, and contented himself by practising with a punt on the Cherwell. There, after repeatedly over balancing himself in the most suicidal manner, he at length peacefully settled down into the lounging blissfulness of a 'Cherwell waterlily'; and on the hot days, among those gentlemen who had moored their punts underneath the overhanging boughs of the willows and limes, and beneath their cool shade were lying, in dolce far niente fashion, with their legs up and a weed in their mouth, reading the last new novel, or some less immaculate work, – among these gentlemen might haply have been discerned the form and spectacles of Mr Verdant Green.

ɔ3

Punting is a much more sedate way to enjoy the delights of the water, as long as you master the technique. Punts were originally designed to ferry goods on the shallow river, but are now used for pleasure. Drifting up the gentle Cherwell, past the grounds of Magdalen and the University Parks, with a picnic and bottle of wine, maybe stopping at the Victoria Arms before turning back: what a wonderful way to spend a summer evening! Let us follow a solitary young lady as she strolls on the banks of the Cherwell ...

Beside her the stream steals along – a soothing, sluggish companion. No song or rush has it, like the flashing northern becks; but what green reflections in it! What long water-weeds, swinging slowly to its slow current! How the willows – pensive almost as olives in their grave dim leafage – have printed themselves on its quiet, silent heart. How riotously green are the fat low meadows that, all winter long, the floods had drowned!

Here, a May-bush has strewn the white largesse of its petals on the water, and there another, less overblown, stoops to look at is own pink face's double. There are two cuckoos: one loud and near, one soft and distant, answering each other across the meads. Beneath the bank at her foot, an undergraduate lies stretched along his boat, with his book. Three others in a punt are waggishly trying to upset each other. She sits down on a bench and idly watches them, till, with shouts of young laughter, they float out of sight. Another punt, a canoe, a skiff, a boat with ladies in it. Her heart jumps.

Ah, no! not her ladies! a boat freighted with hawthorn boughs and guelder-rose branches, that tell of a joyous day's Maying in the country. Endless young gentlemen in flannels, punting, sculling, lying supine.

୧୭

It is also possible to venture further afield; from the town centre to the north and west through the flat common land of Port Meadow and on towards Godstow. This time our young lady is accompanied by the appropriately named, 'Rivers':

Here are no imperative Eights, out of whose way all lesser boats must clear, under penalty of being apostrophized by a ferocious "Look ahead!, sir!" and then run down. And yet there is no lack of company here either, on this splendid summer day.

Above, the pale bright sky, holding her forget-me-not-coloured shield; and below, the windings of the slow broad river, and the great expanse of hedgeless meadow-land. The horses, summering there, stand knee-deep in the stream, eating, or pretending to eat, the weeds; one having a wet roll of utter enjoyment in the shallows. Sheets of little ranunculus are all ablow, each stiff, straight stem and small white, head erect on the water. Countless geese stalk along the meadow, waddling and cropping the grass. Others, like a white fleet, paddle and dive for water weeds.

Into the midst of this feathered Armada they see the larger boat, which has shot ahead of them, being lustily pulled to give it a fright… The geese separate, screeching and oaring away; and one gosling, overtaken by the prow, dives and rises again ten paces away.

Both Rivers and Belinda laugh. There is something healthy and clearing to the moral atmosphere in a joint laugh. Rivers' mirth dies into a long sigh of contentment.

"What a day!" he says, resting on his oars, and staring up at the sky. "I love the river; how I missed it at first! I used to dream about it!"

ೞ

It was on the river in 1862 that C.L. Dodgson (Lewis Carroll)
first created the stories that would become Alice in Wonderland *for the daughters of the Dean of Christchurch. This poem*
describes how it came about:

> All in the golden afternoon,
> Full leisurely we glide;
> For both our oars, with little skill,
> By little arms are plied.
> While little hands make vain pretence
> Our wanderings to guide.

> Ah, cruel Three! In such an hour,
> Beneath such dreamy weather,
> To beg a tale of breath too weak
> To stir the tiniest feather?
> Yet what can one poor voice avail
> Against three tongues together?

Thus grew the tale of Wonderland:
Thus slowly, one by one,
Its quaint events were hammered out
And now the tale is done,
And home we steer, a merry crew,
Beneath the setting sun.

ॐ

Despite the constant idolisation of the city, the effusions of love and veneration with which she has been honoured, it has to be admitted that Oxford has a less than romantic name. Antiquarians and poets throughout the ages seem to have suffered some degree of embarrassment at the mundane origins of the city and have gone to great lengths to establish complex legends of its etymology and history:

In the 1000 and 9th Year before Christ, A.M. 2954, Memphric King of the Britains, (Son of Madan, Son of Locrin, Son of Brutus) is said to have built it; whence it had the name of Caer Memphric; (Caer in the Celtic or British Tongue, signifying a City) Of whom nothing can be said to his Honour, except that he was Father of an hopeful son Ebranc, and founded a noble City called after his own Name. Oxford was first called Mimbre (this being Celtic and British for Memphric to this Day) then Belle-situm, from a pretty mountain near, afterwards Ridohen (q. Rid-ychen) implying in the Celtic language, a Ford of Oxen, and Caer Vosso (meaning Bosso) a Certain Earl that flourished in the time of King Arthur.

This practice was satirised by Thomas Warton in his eighteenth century parody of an Oxford Guide book: The Companion to the Guide and The Guide to the Companion:

Antiquarians, in general, seem to have mistaken the etymology of Bellositum, the reputed Roman name of the City of Oxford. The Rev. Mr. Pointer, in his manuscript notes on Rishanger, who flourished in the reign of Henry the third, writes this word Bulositum, and derives it from the Greek ie: The City of Wisdom. This derivation I cannot entirely approve; but must own, that it has suggested a manner of spelling the word which I take to be right, viz. Bullositum. – Mr Hearne informs us, and indeed the common name Oxford implies the same, "that a part of the river Isis near the town was the most considerable Ford in England for the passage of Oxen." And why not likewise for Bulls? … Why may we not suppose...that the Ford was common to horned cattle in general? Nay that even Cows had more concern in this case than is commonally supposed, seems very probable from the name of the neighbouring village, Cowley …

ଔ

In the words of Anthony Wood:

… however it is, severall authors are not wanting that maintaine Memphric the founder of our city and have with as much credit believed it as the comming Brute into this land which some doe from undeniable grounds defend. As for my owne part, I shall not insist much upon it, forasmuch (as I have elsewhere said) the actions and occurences that were done in those obscure ignorant and disturbed times are chiefly delivered upon aime and conjecture.

ଔ

In his History and Antiquities of the City of Oxford, *Wood recounts the popular legend of the origin of the city's name, based on the triumphant return of the city's patron saint, the saxon princess Frideswide. Frideswide, a nun, had been forced into hiding after being pursued by an amorous Prince. Her aversion to marriage was so great that she even struck the prince blind to avoid being caught. Her return to Oxford was remembered in …*

… an old tradition that goeth from father to son of our inhabitants, which much derogateth from the antiquity of this city.

And that is when Frideswyde had bin soe long absent from hence, she came from Binsey (triumphing with her virginity) into the city mounted on a milk whith ox betokening innocency; and, as she rode along the streets, she would forsooth be still speaking to her ox, 'ox forth', 'ox forth'; or (as 'tis related), 'bos perge' (that is, 'ox goe on' or 'ox (goe on) forth'): and hence they undiscreetly say that our city was from thence called Oxforth or Oxford.

But this name of Oxford, as I have already demonstrated, was knowne long before Frideswyde's time, it being imposed by the Saxons who at their first comming (which was about the year 447 and almost 300 years before the time of which wee are now speaking) altered its old British name *Rid-ychen* (which is 'vadum boum', 'the ford of oxen') to their owne language Oxenford, or Oxford as 'tis written to this day.

A
University
Collage

If the origins of the city have produced such speculation, then the foundation of the University is even more uncertain. Certainly by the twelfth century it was established as a seat of learning, but how this came about is unknown. A favourite myth among eager antiquarians was that the University was started by King Alfred. Up until the nineteenth century, members of University College spuriously claimed the monarch as their founding father in order to assert the seniority of their institution.

When these two schooles [ie. Oxford and Cambridge Universities] should be first builded, and who their original founders, as yet is uncertaine: nevertheless as there is great likelihood that Cambridge was begun by one Cantaber a Spaniard (...) so Alfred is said to be the first beginner of the universitie of Oxford, albeit that I cannot warrant the same to be so yong, sith I find by good authoritie, that John of Beverlie studied in the university Hall at Oxford, which was long before Alfred was either born or gotten...

William Harrison: *Description of England.*

છ

However it came about, it is the University that has made Oxford famous throughout the world and enticed thousands of visitors to the city:

Judging our London Atmosphere grosser, more implete and pregnant with infections and distempering Exhalations than that of the Country; and being highly nauseated with the foetid Emanations of putrified Carcasses: I thought it extremely necessary for my own Preservation, to visit the Rural, Flowry and Delightsome Plains. Having not as yet determined which way I should steer my Course, at last I resolv'd for Oxon: out of great Curiosity to satisfie myself concerning the Customs and Regulations of this so Famous University, the Source of all Learning, Seminary of all Morality, Mother of all Piety and Propagator of all Sobriety and Moderation.

છ

To many outsiders the 'customs and regulations' of the University may well remain something of a mystery. In the eighteenth century play, 'An Oxonian in Town', some Oxford undergraduates leave their august surroundings for the excitement and iniquities of London. In Covent Garden they encounter the Irishman McShuffle, who is curious about the world of academia:

KNOWELL: Why really, gentlemen, this is more free and easy than a moping college life, I must confess: and to be let into the secrets of the knowing ones is a genteeler subsistence, and will introduce one into better company, than all the learning that can be scraped together at the University.

McSHUFFLE: Larning! oh, that must be very stupid! But pray, what do they all do at this shame univarshity?

KNOWELL: Do! why some few unaccountable fellows cultivate the arts and the sciences, and study the languages.

McSHUFFLE: The languages! – Do they understand Irish, honey?

KNOWELL: No, faith; I don't believe any of them are in the least acquainted with it.

McSHUFFLE: Oh, then the devil burn me, if mine own shelf, or Paddy is not a greater Scholar than any of them.

ⓒ

As a young boy Jude is intrigued by the fabled learning of the university he aspires to join:

" ... they never look at anything that folks like we can understand. ..On'y foreign tongues used in the days of the Tower of Babel, when no two families spoke alike. They read that sort of thing as fast as a night-hawk will whir. 'Tis all learning there – nothing but learning, except religion. And that's learning too, for I never could understand it. Yes, 'tis a serious-minded place."

Jude the Obscure

൪

But if the university's academic activities remain a puzzle, it is still possible for a visitor to appreciate the ancient buildings in which they take place.

We first drew up at New College, (a strange name for such an old place, but it was new, I think, sometime since the conquest) and went through its quiet, sunny quadrangles, and into its sunny and shadowy gardens. I am in depair about the architecture of these Oxford colleges; it is so impossible to express them in words. They are themselves – as the architect left them, and as Time has modified and improved them – the expression of an idea, which does not admit of being otherwise expressed, or translated into anythimg else. Those old battlemented walls, around the quadrangles – the Gothic ornaments, and quaint devices – the many gables the towers, the windows, with stone mullions, so very antique, yet some of them adorned with fresh flowers in pots, a very sweet contrast – the ivy, mantling the gray stone – and the infinite repose, both in sunshine and shadow – it is as if half a dozen by-gone centuries had set up their rest here, and as if nothing of the present time ever passed through the deeply recessed arch way that shut in the college from the street.

ଔ

Over a hundred and fifty years before Nathaniel Hawthorne, the indefatigable Celia Fiennes also took in the sights of Oxford. Her grammar and spelling may be unorthodox, but her disingenuous account provides an amusing and succinct summary of the 'Colledges' in her day:

There are severall good Colledges I saw most of ym; Waddom hall is but little; in Trinity Colledge is a fine neate Chapple new made finely painted; Christ Church is the largest Colledge, the Courts large, the buildings large and lofty; in one of the Courts is a tower new built for to hang the Mighty Tom, that bell is of a Large size so great a Weight they were forced to have engines from London to raise it up the tower; there is a fine ring of bells in the Colledge St. Magdalines its just by the river; there is to Maudline Hall (which is a very large and good Cloyster) a very fine gravell walk, two or 3 may walke abreast, and rows of trees on either side, and this is round a water which makes it very pleasant.

St. Johns Colledge had fine gardens and walkes but I did

but just look into it; so I did into kings [sic], and queens Colledges and severall of the rest I looked into; they are much alike in building but none so large as Christ Church Colledge; I was in New Colledge which is very neate but not large, the buildings good, the Chapple very fine; the garden was new-makeing, there is a large bason of water in the middle, there is little walkes and mazes and round mounts for the schollars to divert themselves in.

Corpus Christus Colledge – wch is but small – there I was entertained at supper, and eate of their very good bread and beare which is remarkably the best any where Oxford bread is.

CB

The Colledges each have their own particular style and character. Members of the University are fiercely loyal towards their own colleges and most visitors have their personal favourites. Although C.S. Lewis was an undergraduate at University College he later became a fellow of Magdalen (pronounced 'Maudlin'). In this letter to his father he describes his initial impressions of the college, including the habits of both the deer in the park and the Dons in the common room:

My external surroundings are beautiful beyond compare. To live in the Bishop's Palace at Wells would be good, but could hardly be better than this. My big sitting-room looks north and from it I see nothing, not even a gable or a spire, to remind me that I am in a town. I look down on a stretch of level grass which passes into a grove of immemorial forest trees, at present coloured autumn red. Over this stray the deer. They are erratic in their habits. Some mornings when I look out there will be half a dozen chewing the cud just underneath me, and on others there will be none in sight – or one little stag (not much bigger than a calf and looking too slender for the weight of his antlers) standing still and sending through the fog that queer little bark which is these beasts' 'moo'. It is a sound that will soon be as familiar to me as the cough of the cows in the field at home, for I hear it day and night. On my right hand as I look from these windows is 'his favourite walk' (Addison's). My smaller sitting room and bedroom look out southwards across a broad lawn to the main buildings of Magdalen with the tower beyond it …

As to the 'College' in the other sense - as a human society - I can say little yet. One's first impressions of a new set are changed many times in the first month. They are all very nice to me. The general tone of the place strikes me as rather slack and flippant - I mean among the Dons - but I may well be mistaken...The most surprising thing is that they are much less formal than Univ. They don't dress for dinner except when the President dines, on which occasion a warning notice is sent round to our rooms. Again, there are an enormous number of us compared with Univ., and we meet much more often. Thus we breakfast and lunch in the Common Room; meals in your own rooms (which I had thought universal at Oxford) being unknown here, either for Dons or undergraduates. The latter are a little aloof from the rest of Oxford; not entirely through affectation but because as a matter of geography we are 'at the town's end'; or as someone said, we are at the beginning of Suburbia ...

☃

In A Week at Oxford, *the anonymous but obliging narrator accompanies his new acquaintances on a stroll around 'Maudlin-Walks.' The attractions of the natural scene are outstripped in this extract by the flowery prose and fertile adjectives:*

The weather being mighty Clear and Serene they were very earnest to refresh themselves with a pleasant Walk. I tender'd my service and promised to show them the finest walk as 'tis reported in the whole Kingdom. They told me 'twould be esteemed no small Favour, if I would oblige them with my Company; I granted their request and accordingly show'd them to Maudlin-Walks. The young gentleman said he thought they were adorn'd with all things requisite to render them extremely Delightsome. He protested that he never saw more exact position and order of Trees Rivetted thro'out the whole Walk. That he never beheld a more Verdant and Flowery Meadow; he extoll'd the contrivance of the Ground, its easy Ascents and Degradations, its Smoothness, its Well-Proportioned Latitude and Moderate Length. The pleasure occasioned by the Murmuring Noise of the Adjacent River he thought extremely Ravishing and Delightsome. To see the

Fishes Besporting themselves in their proper Element, Decoy'd and Caught by the vigilant and dextrous Angler was accounted by him pleasant Interruptions and Diverting delays in Walking.

ଓ

Magdalen is also the site for Oxford's celebration of May-Morning. At dawn, choristers from Magdalen College School climb the college tower and sing to the rising sun, morris-men dance in the High Street and Magdalen Bridge is packed with people:

If we were ever in Oxford on the morning of the first of May we should rise out of our beds in the cold grey dawn and come here at five o'clock to hear the choristers greeting the sun from the top of the tall tower, which is one of the glories of Oxford.

Mr Bent says that he has never missed a year since he came up.

He described the wonder of it – the long climb up the tower, the coming out into the morning mists, the burst of song just as the sun rises, the clashing of the glorious Magdalen bells which seem to sway the slender tower. Then caps and gowns are thrown wildly in the air, and helter-skelter rush the choir-boys down the ladders and the stairs. Then off to the meadows to pick the fritillaries, or up Headington Hill to look down on Oxford lying below in the dewy meadows. Some day we too will come, will we not, to greet the sun on May-Day?

Maida Stanier, the wife of the Master of Magdalen College School, offers a less idealistic view of proceedings in her 'Madrigal for May-Morning':

Now is the month of Maying,
Now Phoebus gins arise –
See where the laggard choristers
Half-ope their bleary eyes,
With a toor-a-lay and titti-fol,
They groan and ope their eyes.

The lark now leaves his wat'ry nest,
And loude sings cuckoo –
A grumbling Dean climbs up the Tower
And blows on fingers blue.
With a ring-a-ding and a nonny-no,
He blows on fingers blue.

Now skip the gartered Morrisers
To tabor's merry din –
Strephon is peering from a punt
At Chloe fallen in,
O willow, willow, a tish-oo,
At Chloe fallen in.

Golden the daffadillies
The wanton zephyrs toss
That silver swan and Chloe

Both look distinctly cross.
Twang, twang, a-diddle-o,
Both look distinctly cross.

The westron wind is blowing,
The small rain down doth rain
O, love that I were out of this
And in my bed again,
Alack-a-day and well away
And in my bed again.

Hark, now the joyous anthem
Goes spiralling around –
So does that plane. I never heard –
Did you? – the music's sound.
O waly, waly, dash it all,
I never heard a sound.

Fie then, why sit we musing?
Good cause have we for cheer
Summer's i-cumen in. We need
Not bother for a year
To sing a merry roundelay,
With fa-la-la and Shepherds' hey,
To celebrate the first of May,
Thank goodness, for a year.

 G8

Arguably the grandest of the Oxford colleges is Christ Church.
Founded by Thomas Wolsey as Cardinal College in 1525, it
was taken over by Henry VIII when Wolsey fell from royal
favour. Henry converted the ancient priory of St. Frideswide,
that lay on the site, into the City Cathedral, and the college
was renamed Christ Church. A sixteenth century play
remembers the college's original founder:

> A College fair in Oxford I did make,
> A sumptuous house, a stately work indeed,
> I gave great lands to that, for learning's sake,
> To bring up youth, and succour scholar's need.
> That charge of mine full many a mouth did feed,
> When I in Court was seeking some good turn
> To mind my torch or make my candle burn.

> (Thomas Churchyard, 1520-1604:
> 'The Tragedy of Cardinal Wolsey')

ଔ

Over the west entrance to the college is Tom Tower, designed
by Sir Christopher Wren to house the bell that had hung in
Osney Abbey. The Abbey was dissolved during the
Reformahon and today nothing remains of its former glory
apart from Great Tom:

> Be dumb ye infant chimes, thump not the metal
> That ne'er outrung a tinker and his kettle,

Cease all your petty larums, for today
Is young Tom's resurrection from the clay:
And know, when Tom shall ring his loudest knells
The big'st of you'll be thought but dinner bells.
Rejoice with Christ Church – look higher Oseney,
Of giant bells the famous treasury;
The base vast thundering Clock of Westminster,–
Grave Tom of Lincoln and huge Excester
Are but Tom's eldest brothers, and perchance
He may call cousin with the bell of France.

It was Great Tom that Jude heard during his first evening walk around Oxford. He didn't miscount the number of chimes: the bell tolls one hundred and one times every night at five past nine (nine o' clock on the Oxford meridian); one chime for each of the original students of the college.

ೞ

During the English Civil War, King Charles I resided at Christ Church. The presence of the court greatly altered the atmosphere of the seventeenth century City and University, as this extract from the romance, 'John Inglesant' describes.

The ancient colleges and halls were thronged with ladies and courtiers; noblemen lodged in small attics over bakers' shops in the streets; soldiers were quartered in the college gates and in the kitchens; yet, with all this confusion, there was maintained both something of a courtly pomp, and something of a learned and religious society. The King dined and supped in public, and walked in state in Christ Church meadow and Merton Gardens and the Grove of Trinity, which the wits called Daphne. A parliament sat from day to day; service was sung daily in all the Chapels; books both of learning and poetry were printed in the city; and the distinctions which the colleges had to offer were conferred with pomp on the royal followers, as almost the only rewards the King had to bestow ... gay courtiers and gayer ladies jostled old and severe divines and college heads, and crusty tutors used the sarcasms they had been wont to hurl at their pupils to reprove the ladies whose conduct appeared to them at least far from decorous. Christmas interludes were enacted in Hall, and Shakespeare's plays performed by the King's players, assisted by amateur performers ... The groves and walks of the colleges, and especially Christ Church meadow and the Grove at Trinity, were the resort of this gay and brilliant throng; the woods were vocal with song and music, and love and gallantry sported themselves along the pleasant river banks. The poets and wits vied with each other in classic conceits and parodies, wherein the events of the day and every individual incident were portrayed and satirized. Wit, learning, and religion, joined hand in hand, as in some grotesque and brilliant masque.

ᗡ

As old as the University itself, has been its constant rivalry with 'the Other Place'; an irresolvable contest based, needless to say, on loyalty and prejudice rather than anything else. Oxonians will be pleased to note however, that the apparently unbiassed observer, Karl Baedeker, favoured Oxford over Cambridge in his first guide to Great Britain in 1887:

Oxford is on the whole more attractive than Cambridge to the ordinary visitor, and the traveller is therefore recommended to visit Cambridge first, or omit it altogether if he cannot visit both.

ßß

The chronicler, William Harrison, is unusual in his commitment to both camps and gets in rather a tangle by trying to share out his praise between them.

Of these two [Universities], that of Oxford, which lieth west and by north of London, standeth the most pleasantly, being invironed in maner round about with woods on the hills aloft, and goodlie rivers in the bottoms and vallies beneath, whose courses would breed no small commoditie to that citie and countrie about, if such impediments were remooved as greatlie annoie the same, and hinder the cariage which might be made thither also from London ... The colleges of Oxford, for curious workmanship and privat commodities, are much more statelie, magnificent, and commodious than those of Cambridge: and thereunto the streets of the towne for the most part more large and comelie...But for uniformitie of building, orderlie compaction, and politicke regiment, the towne of Cambridge, as the newer workmanship, exceedeth that of Oxford (which otheroise is and hath beene the greater of the two) by manie a fold (as I gesse) although I know diverse that are of the contrarie opinion. This also is certaine, that whatsoever the difference in building of the towne streets, the townesmen of both are glad when they may match and annoie the students, by incroching upon their liberties, and keepe them bare by extreame sale of their wares, whereby manie of them become rich for a time, but afterward fall againe into povertie, bicause that goods evill gotten doo seldome long indure … In all other things there is so great equalitie betweene these two universities, as no man can imagine how to set down any greater; so that they seem to be the bodie of one well ordered commonwealth, onelie divided by distance of place, and not in friendlie consent of orders. In speaking therefore of one, I can not but describe the other; and in commendation of the first, I can not but extoll the latter; and so much the rather, for that they are both so deere unto me, as that I can not readilie tell unto whether of them I owe the most good will.

☙

In more extreme style, Anthony Wood leaves no doubt as to where his loyalty lies!

Oxford … [was] … a famous place before this present Town of Cambridge in all probability was built, and whilst the brutest of all beasts, viz. Hogs and Pigs lay wallowing and grunting in the gronnae, mire, fennish places or sloughs …

where the said town now standeth ... Certain it is, that diverse
... scholars went to Cambridge, and there read and planted
the same Oxonian doctrine, that they had here received; which
as a pleasant stream, did afterward water and soil those parts
with true learning, making thereby that place once again ...
an Oxford colony.

☙

*The university has excited extremes of emotion from all who
encounter it either as students or visitors. It seems impossible
to be merely indifferent to its appearance, learning and
traditions; you either love it or hate it. Some visitors have
been sceptical:*

EMPEROR OF SAXONY:

> Trust me, Plantagenet, these Oxford schooles
> Are richly seated neere the riverside:
> The mountains full of fat and fallow deere,
> The bathing pastures laid with kine and flocks,
> The towne gorgeous with high built colledges,
> And scholars seemely in their grave attire,
> Learned in searching principles of art.
> What is thy judgement, Jacquis Vandermast?

VANDERMAST (A GERMAN SCHOLAR):

> That lordly are the buildings of the towne,
> Spatious the romes and full of pleasant walkes:
> But for the doctors, how that they be learned,
> It may be meanly, for ought I can heere.

While others have been downright outraged:

Upon beholding the masses of buildings, at Oxford, devoted to what they call *'learning'*, I could not help reflecting on the drones that they contain and the wasps that they send forth! However, malignant as some are, the great and prevalent characteristic is *folly*: emptiness of head; want of talent; and one-half of the fellows who are what they call *educated* here, are unfit to be clerks in the grocer's or mercer's shop. - As I looked up at what they call *University Hall*, I could not help reflecting that what I had written, even since I left Kensington on the 29th of October, would produce more effect, and do more good in the world, than all that had for a hundred years, been written by all the members of the University, who devour, perhaps, not less than *a million pounds a year*, arising from property, completely at the disposal of the "Great Council of the Nation"; and I could not help exclaiming to myself: "Stand forth, ye big-wigged, ye gloriously feeding Doctors! Stand forth, ye rich of that church whose poor have had given them *a hundred thousand pounds a year*, not out of your riches, but out of the taxes, raised, in part, from the salt of the labouring man! Stand forth and face me, who have, from the pen of my leisure hours, sent, amongst your flocks, a hundred thousand sermons in ten months! More than you have all done for the last half century!" I exclaimed in vain. I dare say (for it was at peep of day) that not a man of them had yet endeavoured to unclose his eyes.

ભ

Perhaps it was to be expected that the vitriolic William Cobbett would work himself up into a frenzy of italics and exclamation marks at the wealth and privileges of the university, but it is not only visitors that have expressed such disapproval of the place. In the following extracts a seventeenth century professor and an eighteenth century undergraduate vent their antipathy:

As to Dr. Pococks place, it was offered me and I refused it, and that for two reasons; the first is, I nauseate that learning, and am resolved to loose noe more time upon it; and the second is, I nauseate Christchurch; and, further, if I should goe to Oxford again I must quit whatever I have here, and the advantage would scarce pay for the remove. But my main argument is, I have an unconquerable aversion to the place, and will never live more among such people who now have the prevailing power there.

Sir Humphrey Prideaux to John Ellis: Letter 12.10.1691

To the University of Oxford I acknowledge no obligation; and she will as cheerfully renounce me for a son, as I am willing to disclaim her for a mother. I spent fourteen months at Magdalen College; they proved the fourteen months the most idle and unprofitable of my whole life …
… The schools of Oxford and Cambridge were founded in a dark age of false and barbarous science; and they are still tainted with the vices of their origin. Their primitive discipline was adapted to the education of priests and monks; and the

government still remains in the hands of the clergy, an order of men whose manners are remote from the present world, and whose eyes are dazzled by the light of philosophy...

Memoirs of my Life

ଓ

The ungrateful author of this piece is Edward Gibbon, who matriculated at Magdalen aged fourteen, but was forced to leave the University a year later after declaring himself a Roman Catholic.

ଓ

In Oxford From Within, *a writer sits down to record his feelings about Oxford and its University, but his work is interrupted by the intrusion of an angry visitor:*

"Alma mater, home of lost causes, whispering the last enchantments of the Middle Ages." The industrious writer dreamed.

"A stagnant marsh of useless knowledge, withdrawn from the flowing river of life; where young men learn to be prigs and are inoculated with the poison of respectability: where the Medusa head of tradition is polished to slay the sons of Progress. Kindly mother of curates and schoolmasters and dons: a step-mother to poets. A place of sloth and superiority: a trap baited by the beauty of old buildings: a prop for institutions which are moribund and spread the odour of decay throughout the life of the country." The violent intruder shouted. A sad grave eye was fixed upon him. That was his only answer. Accordingly he continued;

"It is supposed to be the home of learning, but the learning is of such an order that the rich and the athletic are alone respected. Taste for the right thing in waistcoats or caps is cultivated more surely than a taste for the right thing in science or literature or art. It has no proper values, and having no proper values, it may teach young men how to become pedants or cricketers, but it cannot teach them how to live."

"You are speaking," said the industrious writer, "against youth and against learning; not so much against Oxford as the people who live in Oxford."

"The two are inseparable," fumed the intruder.

"Would you annhilate the place?" his friend mildly persisted, or would you slaughter all young men – another and a vaster massacre of the innocents – and destroy learning root and branch out of the land?" So they tussled it out. Two such people often inhabit one and the same man.

☙

The Bodleian Library

Let us leave these two alter egos to argue amongst themselves and turn our attention to the Bodleian Library, one of the oldest and largest libraries in Europe. Henry V's brother Duke Humphrey of Gloucester founded a library for the University in the fifteenth century with an endowment of books that were housed above the Divinity School, but by the end of the sixteenth century this library had fallen into disrepair. Let Defoe explain further:

In this state of Things, one Sir *Thomas Bodley*, a Wealthy and Learned Knight, Zealous for the Encouragement both of Learning and Religion, resolv'd to apply, both his time, and Estate, to the Erecting and Furnishing a New Library for the publick use of the University.

In this Good and Charitable undertaking, he went on so

successfully, for so many Years, and with such a profusion of Expence, and obtain'd such Assistances from all the Encouragers of Learning in his time, that having collected Books and Manuscripts from all Parts of the Learned World; he got leave of the University, (*and well they might grant it*) to place them in the old Library Room, built as is said, by the good Duke *Humphry*.

ભ

Sir Thomas Bodley's decision to restore and extend the library was greeted with expressions of joy and gratitude by his contemporaries:

Most noble Bodley! we are bound to thee
For no smal part of our eternity.
Thy treasure was not spent on Horse and Hound
Nor that new mode, which doth old States confound;
Thy legacies another way did go:
Nor were they left to those would spend them so.
Thy safe discreet Expence on us did flow;
Walsam is in the midst of Oxford now.
Th'hast made us all thine Heirs: whatever we
Herafter write, 'tis thy Posterity.
This is thy Monument! here thou shalt stand
Till the times fail in their last grain of Sand.
And wheresoe're thy silent Reliques keep,
This tomb will never let thine Honour sleep.
Still we shall think upon thee; all our fame

Meets here to speak one Letter of thy name.
Thou canst not dye! here thou art more safe
Where every Book is thy large Epitaph.

Henry Vaughan, 1638:
'On Sir Thomas Bodley's Library'

✑

Authors seek ye? 'Ready before your eyes!'
Each classic author in his bookcase cries.
Of this great work, scarce parallelled on earth,
Seek ye the Founder? Bodley gave it birth.

John Owen: *Epigrams*, 1612.

✑

The Bodleian lies on the North side of Radcliffe Square. With the dome of the Radcliffe Camera at its centre, this is possibly the most beautiful and distinctive place in Oxford and is consequently endlessly reproduced for the tourists on postcards and calenders, bookcovers and tea-towels:

… In the soft late spring air a haze of peaceful antiquity seemed to permeate the very stones of the buildings. The round dominating dome of the Camera in the centre; the St. Mary's spire; the dull yellow wall of Brasenose; the twin towers of All Souls; the Bodleian; Hertford and Exeter Colleges – all seemed to be taking part in a solemn atmospheric ceremonial service.

Chiang Yee: *The Silent Traveller.*

ભ

In this harmonious setting, the Bodleian is one of the centrepieces of any tour of Oxford and magnificent enough to impress even the most distinguished visitors. On one of his trips to Oxford, King James I is reported to have remarked:

If I were not a King I would be a University man; and if it were that I must be a prisoner, if I might have my wish, I would have no other prison than this library, and be chained together with these good authors.

(recorded by Robert Burton in *The Anatomy of Melancholy*)

ભ

In the following extracts, a variety of other visitors down the ages express their own reactions. First, an Edwardian lady:

Never went I before into such a very paradise of books. The atmosphere seemed to be composed of the thoughts and feelings of centuries of book-lovers … 'Profoundly blessed,' thought I, 'must be the people who sit here all day long and read; surely learning must steal into their minds if it is not already there; surely the least grateful amongst them and the least reverent must send up a little psalm of praise and thanksgiving when his eye lights upon Bodley's portrait, and his thoughts go back over all that Bodley did for the lover of books.' Happy readers! Thrice happy librarians! How I envied a girl who was consulting a volume of the mighty catalogue. She had a little air of wisdom and aloofness from the world which was infinitely charming. I dare say that really she is not a bit cleverer than any other girl. I dare say that she has long ceased to feel the special charm of her surroundings, and to remember what a lucky girl she is.

... a member of the Italian court of Cosimo III:

The members of this University have so great a value for their library, that they prefer it, both as to the number and rarity of its books, to that of the Vatican, persuading themselves that there is none in Europe to be compared with it: but, considering it dispassionately, it does not contain so numerous or such scarce books, as to deserve the praise of being the only library, or the most considerable one in the world, there being many others which are equall and even superior to it.

Travels of Cosimo

... and, finally, a seventeeth century visitor from the country:

A Door I spy'd was open standing,
I budged no further than my Band in:
But by a Schollard I was holp in,
A Civil Youth, and a well spoken;
We went together up the Stair-case,
Going, till coming to a rare-place
As thick of Books as one could thatch 'um,
And Ladders stood about to reach 'um ...
I ask'd a young Youth what it mean'd,
That all them Conjuring Books are chain'd:
Hoa said they being full of Cunning,
It sems would else have been for running,
Before they had them Chains, they say,
A number of them run away.
There's such an Oceant still, I wonder'd,
How they could miss a thousand hunder'd.
But that indeed again is something,
They can know all things by the round thing.
As I went on, the Folks that reads,
Would many times pop up their Heads.
And douck 'um down (may hap) again,
And these are call'd the Learned Men.
And look for all the world as frighted,
But were I to be hang'd, or knighted,
I can't imagine what mought ail'd 'um,
For could they think one wou'd a steal'd 'um;
Well, by and by, there' s one comes to me,
I though the fellow might have knew me,

Hoa said, I must not make a stomping,
And that it was no place to jump in;
Whop Sir, thought I, and what ado's here,
About the Nails that in ones Shoes are;
Hoa told me that the Men were earning,
A world of something by their Learning,
And that a Noise might put then out,
So that they ne're could bring't about.

ജ

Many people would argue that the atmosphere of the Bodleian in the twentieth century is not very different. 'The folks that reads' are a distinctive breed, as much a part of the library, as the books in which they are buried. Despite the extent of the modern Bodleian, Duke Humphrey's library, almost unchanged since Bodley's day, remains at its heart. It is perhaps not surprising then, that readers in this ancient room come to be affected (one way or the other) by the learned serenity of their surroundings:

I spend all my mornings in the Bodleian ... If only one could smoke and if only there were upholstered chairs, this would be one of the most delightful places in the world. I sit in 'Duke Humphrey's Library', the oldest, a Fifteenth Century building with a very beautiful wooden painted ceiling above me and a little mullioned window on my left hand through which I look down on the garden of Exeter, where these mornings I see the sudden squalls of wind and rain driving the first blossoms off the fruit trees and snowing the lawn with them … This room … is full of books which stand in little cases at right angles to the wall, so that between each pair there is a kind of little 'box' – in the public-house sense of the word – and in these boxes one sits and reads. By a merciful provision, however many books you send for, they will be left on your chosen table at night for you to resume work next morning; so that one gradually accumulates a pile as comfortably as in one's own room. There is not, as in modern libraries, a forbidding framed notice to shriek 'Silence'; on the contrary the more moderate request, 'Talk little and tread lightly'. There is indeed always a faint murmur going on of semi whispered conversations in the neighbouring boxes. It disturbs no one. I rather like to hear the hum of the hive …

As you may imagine, one sees many oddities amongst one's fellow readers – people whom I have never met elsewhere and who look as if they were shut up with the other properties every night. Positively the only drawback is that beauty, antiquity and overheating weave a spell very much more suited to dreaming than to working. But I trust in time to become inoculated. (The practice of opening the window in one's box is not, I need hardly say, encouraged.)

○3

The building that houses the Bodleian was originally the examinations schools, as the signs over the arched doorways remind us. In the sequel to Tom Brown's Schooldays, *Thomas*

Hughes gives an account of the nerve-racking atmosphere of the School's quadrangle before a University exam.

There is no more characteristic spot in Oxford then the quadrangle of the schools ... Since alma mater has ceased to take cognizance of 'treasons, insurrections, felonies, and mayhem,' it is here in that fateful and inexorable quadrangle, and the buildings which surround it, that she exercises her most potent spells over the spirits of her children. I suppose that a man being tried for his life must be more uncomfortable than an undergraduate being examined for his degree, and that to be hung – perhaps even to be pilloried – must be worse then to be plucked. But after all, the feelings in both cases must be essentially the same, only more intense in the former; and an institution that can examine a man (in literis humanioribus, in humanities so called) once a year for two or three days at a time, has nothing to complain of, though it has no longer the power of hanging him at once out of hand.

The Students

And what of the people who have to undergo this ordeal? The students of Oxford are famed in theory for their learning and academic achievements. In practice their reputations have, more often than not, been based on less lofty pursuits.

" ... I have heard that there is a great deal of wine drank in Oxford."

"Oxford! There is no drinking at Oxford now, I assure you. Nobody drinks there. You would hardly meet with a man who goes beyond his four pints at the utmost. Now, for instance, it was reckoned a remarkable thing at the last party in my rooms, that upon average we cleared about five pints a head. It was looked upon as something out of the common way. Mine is famous good stuff to be sure. You would not often meet with anything like it in Oxford – and that may account for it. But this will give you a notion of the general rate of drinking there."

"Yes, it does give a notion," said Catherine warmly, "and that is, that you all drink a great deal more wine than I thought you did."

Jane Austen: *Northanger Abbey*

ଔ

The earliest description of an Oxford student is Chaucer's 'Clerk of Oxenford' in the Prologue to The Canterbury Tales.

A clerk there was of Oxenford also,
That unto logyk hadde long ygo.
As lene was his hors as is a rake,
And he was nat right fat, I undertake,
But loked holwe, and thereto soberly.
Ful thredbar was his overeste courtepy;
For he hadde geten him yet no benefice,
Ne was so worldly for to have office.
For hym levere have at his beddes heed
Twenty bookes, clad in blak or reed,
Of Aristotle and his philosophie,
Than robes riche, or fithele, or gay sautrie.
But al be that he was a philosophre,
Yet hadde he but litel gold in cofre;
But al that he myghte of his freendes hente,
On bookes and on lernynge he it spente,
And bisily gan for the soules preye

Of hem that yaf hym wherewith to scoleye.
Of studie took he moost cure and moost heede.
Noght o word spak he moore than was neede,
And that was seyd in forme and reverence,
And short and quyk, and ful of hy sentence;
Sownynge in moral vertu was his speche,
And gladly wolde he lerne, and gladly teche.

ᘓ

The following extracts describe the character of Oxford students through the centuries. As the university matured, the learning and poverty of Chaucer's Clerk gradually gave way to the decadence of the eighteenth century, the self-satisfaction of Victorian Oxford and the doomed hedonism of the 1920's, supremely and famously captured in Evelyn Waugh's Brideshead Revisited.

ACADEMIA: Seventeenth Century

Now being arrived at his Colledge,
The place of Learning, and of Knowledge,
A while he'll leer about, and snivel ye,
And doff his hat to all most civilly,
Being told at home that a shame Face too,
Was a great sign he had some Grace too,
He'l speak to none, alas! for he's
Amaz'd at every man he sees:
May-hap this lasts a Week, or two,

Till some Scab laughs him out on't, so
That when most you'd expect his mending,
His Breeding's ended, and not ending:
Now he dares walk abroad, and dare ye,
Hat on, in People Faces stare ye,
Thinks what a Fool he was before, to
Pull off his Hat, which he'd no more do;
But that the Devil shites disasters,
So that he's forced to cap the Masters,
He might have nailed it to his Head, else,
And wore it Night, and Day a Bed, else,
And then de'e see, for I'de have you mind it,
He had always known where to find it;

ca

STREPHON'S REVENGE, Eighteenth Century

A College-Smart is a character, which few perhaps are
acquainted with; He is one that spends his Time in a constant
Circle of Engagements and Assignations; He rises at ten,
tattles over his Tea-Table till Twelve, Dines, Dresses; waits
upon his Mistress, drinks Tea again, flutters about in Publick
'till it is dark, then to the Tavern, knocks into College at Two
in the Morning, sleeps till Ten again, and disposes of the
following Day, just as he did of the last: He affects great
Company, and scrapes Acquaintances with golden Tufts and
brocaded Gowns; and after a course of Studies of this Nature

for three or four Years, he huddles over publick Exercises, disputes and passes Examination in the Sciences after the modern Fashion, without understanding a word of what like a Parrot, he is taught memorially to utter; He then canvasses and obtains his Grace amongst the Ladies, and takes his Degree with uncommon Marks of Honour; and thus passes for a most profound Scholar, meerly by being an arrant Blockhead. This Class of Men is very numerous amongst us, and daily encreases without Controul, to the great Scandal and Discredit of all useful Learning, and is an Enormity of very bad Consequence, as it may in time sap the Foundation of the most famous and flourishing Universities in the World.

ೞ

THE LOUNGER

I rise about nine, get to breakfast by ten,
Blow a tune on my flute, or perhaps make a pen;
Read a play till eleven, or cock my lac'd hat;
Then step to my neighbours, 'till dinner, to chat.
Dinner over, to *Tom's* or to *James's* I go,
The news of the town so impatient to know;
While *Law, Locke*, and *Newton*, and all the rum race,
That talk of their modes, their ellipses, and space,
The seat of the soul, and new systems on high,
In holes, as abstruse as their mysteries, lie.
From the coffee-house then I to tennis away,

And at five I post back to my college to pray:
I sup before eight, and secure from all duns,
Undauntedly march to the Mitre or Tuns;
Where in punch or good claret my sorrows I drown,
And toss off a bowl " To the best in the town ;"
At one in the morning, I call what's to pay,
Then home to my college I stagger away;
Thus I tope all the night, as I trifle all day.

ଔ

ENGLISH NOTEBOOKS: Nineteenth century

I ordered luncheon - some cold beef (which Julian and I found
remarkably good) and some ale, which was not so much to
my liking. By-and-by, two or three young men came in, in
wide awake hats, and loose, blouse-like, summerish garments;
and from their talk, I found them to be students of the
University, although their topics of conversation were almost
entirely horses and boats. One of them sat down to the cold
beef and a tankard of ale; the other two drank a tankard of ale
together and went away without paying for it – rather to the
waiter's discontent. Students are very much alike, all the
world over, and, I suppose, in all time; but doubt whether
many of my fellows at college would have gone off without
paying for their beer.

ଔ

BRIDESHEAD REVISITED: Twentieth century

Towards the end of that summer term. I received the last visit and Grand Remonstrance of my cousin Jasper...

'... I expected you to make some mistakes in your first year. We all do ... But you, my dear Charles, whether you realise it or not, have gone straight, hook line and sinker, into the very worst set in the University ... They think because they've got a lot of money to throw about, they can do anything.

'And that's another thing. I don't know what allowance my uncle makes you, but I don't mind betting you're spending double. All *this*,' he said, including in a wide sweep of his hand the evidence of the profligacy about him. It was true; my room had cast its austere winter garments, and, by not very slow stages, assumed a richer wardrobe. 'Is *that* paid for?' (the box of a hundred cabinet Paragas on the sideboard) 'or *those*?' (a dozen frivolous, new books on the table) 'or those?' (a Lalique decanter and glasses) 'or that peculiarly noisome object?' (a human skull lately purchased from the School of Medicine, which, resting in a bowl of roses, formed at the moment, the chief decoration of my table. It bore the motto '*Et in Arcadia ego*' inscribed on its forehead.)

'Yes,' I said, glad to be clear of one charge. 'I had to pay cash for the skull.'

'You can't be doing any work. Not that that matters, particularly if you're making something of your career elsewhere – but are you? Have you spoken at the Union or at any of the clubs? Are you connected with any of the magazines? Are you even making a position in the OUDS?

'And drink – no one minds a man getting tight once or twice a term. In fact, he ought to, on certain occasions. But I hear you're constantly seen drunk in the middle of the afternoon.'

"I'm sorry, Jasper," I said. "I know it must be embarrassing for you, but I happen to *like* this bad set. I *like* getting drunk at luncheon, and though I haven't yet spent quite double my allowance, I undoubtedly shall before the end of term. I usually have a glass of champagne about this time. Will you join me?"

ℭ

In the nineteenth century the first women's colleges were founded at Oxford: Lady Margaret Hall and Somerville. Situated on the outskirts of the city they remained on the very edge of University life until well into the twentieth century. Strict regulations kept the male and female students apart and it was not until 1920 that women were able to obtain a degree:

"… we can't consider ourselves the centre of the University system, for we are not, as a matter of fact, members of the University at all."

Then they told us of the battle that raged some years ago over the question of admitting women to the degree. It must have been a most exciting time. The air of Oxford was thick with pamphlets and leaflets, which were addressed by members of the University to themselves and to the public. Some gave weighty reasons for and against the granting of the degree; some were really witty, some merely silly. One … accused the women of wishing 'to hang on to the skirts of a male University.'

Peaceful households were divided by this burning question, and the subject had to be tabooed at social gatherings, so deeply did it stir the passions of men and women. In some instances the husband gave his vote and interest to the women's cause, while the wife used tongue and energy against it. Some of the more morose and jaundiced sort hinted that the original mistake was made when the University admitted women to its examinations at all.

"We always knew how it would be", they cried. "Women are an ungrateful, discontented, grasping sex. It is never safe to give them anything." And they talked of the thin end of wedges, and of those who take ells when inches have been granted to them...

The great debate came off on the 3rd of March 1896. The motion was lost by an overwhelming majority. It does seem not a little absurd to the observer that a young woman who has taken a high honours should not have a degree, while the silliest little passman who can just scrape through the Schools should be able to write B.A. after his name …

The undergraduates here seem to have been very little moved by the great struggle.

Miss Smith said that a worthy young man once said to her, "It would make a man look rather a fool, don't you know, if his sister came up here and took a first and he got a plough, don't you see?" Such a thing has, I believe been known to happen.

ભ

Despite their inferior position in the eyes of their male counterparts, women eventually managed to become full and involved members of the University; enjoying the privileges of Oxford perhaps all the more because of the difficulties they had faced in obtaining them:

On the whole it was a good place, Oxford: people by the score, possessiveness indulged in having one's own room, romance in wearing cap and gown. She had kept them on all day after being matriculated, looking at herself in all the shop windows as she went home, and carefully sitting opposite her mirror in the afternoon, when, as it was pouring with cold rain and she had done no work, she sat doing Virgil in her room.

And a good place too, in the sun, when she was suddenly consumed with an enthusiam for sculling, and bicycled daily through muddy fields to where the roof of the boat house glowed clear red in the distance against pale and genial skies. She loved to launch the boat: to get in, to try and keep time; the smell of her wet hands in the sun; to be sworn at by the little, pretty, choleric second year girl who took them; to be cold and exhausted: to come home again through air that smelled of bonfires to a large and sleepy tea in hall, where red sunsets shone in at the long windows.

Everything was very fine and clear and cold and golden, in the morning, bicycling to lectures: in the afternoon, sculling: in the evening, looking from her window at the end of the light: one caught one's breath sometimes with the desire for vivid remembrance, for keeping every minute solid, sharp, clear cut, actual, forever.

A good place.

cs

Of course, as well as the students there are the Dons; not, I hasten to add, an exclusive club for gentlemen with the same Christian name, but the illustrious university teachers who try to convert fresh young eighteen year-olds into responsible, scholarly adults ... Although perhaps, on second thoughts, it is an exclusive club after all ...

People talk about the Oxford manner and the Oxford life and the Oxford God knows what else, as if the undergraduates had anything to do with it ... The real Oxford is a close corporation of jolly, untidy, lazy, good-for nothing, humorous old-men, who have been electing their own successors ever since the world began and who intend to go on with it. They'll squeeze under the Revolution or leap over it when the time comes, don't you worry. When I think how little chance I have of ever fighting my way into that unassuming but impregnable fortress, that modest unremoveability, that provokingly intangible stone wall, I think of Keats's poison
Brewed in monkish cell to thin the scarlet
conclave of old men.

Edward Gibbon had some comments on the state of teaching in his day:

The monks of my time were decent easy men, who supinely enjoyed the gifts of the founder; their days were filled by a series of uniform employments; the chapel and the hall, the coffee house and the common-room, till they retired, weary and well satisfied, to a long slumber ... Their conversation stagnated in a round of college business, Tory politics, personal anecdotes and private scandal ...

The first tutor into whose hands I was resigned appears to have been one of the best of the tribe: Dr. Waldegrave was a learned and pious man, of a mild disposition, strict morals and abstemious life, who seldom mingled in the politics or the jollity of the college. But his knowledge of the world was confined to the University; his learning was of the last, rather than the present age; his temper was indolent; his faculties, which were not of the first rate, had been relaxed by the climate, and he was satisfied, like his fellows, with the slight and superficial discharge of an important trust ...

After the departure of Dr. Waldegrave, I was transferred, with his other pupils, to his academical heir, whose literary character did not command the respect of the college. Dr. [Winchester] well remembered that he had a salary to receive, and only forgot that he had a duty to perform.

❃

Not content with chronicling the history of the city, and the University, and keeping a journal of contemporary Oxford life, Anthony Wood also collected a series of witty (?) anecdotes about the seventeenth century University and its characters into a book entitled Modius Salium. *This section concludes with some of its entries:*

Two Scholars resolving to study very hard, agreed to lock each other in their studies.

Tom Hill, Student of Christ Church, a great Eater, was reported to have eaten a Pound of Candles, and forthwith to have spewed up his Lights.

Epitaph for Merideth, Organist of New College: "Here lies one blown out of Breath, Who liv'd a-merry Life, and dy'd a Merry Death"

Dr. Kettle, President of Trinity College, used to show how to make a triangle in a square thus: Bring a Pig into the College Quadrangle, there set the college Dog on the Pig to soule or lug it; while the Dog holds the Pig by the Ear, take the Tail of the Pig in one Hand, and the Tail of the Dog in the other. So there's a triangle in a square.

"Magdalen College Grove would make a better Grove if the Trees were cut down"; quoth Dr. John Wilkinson Principal of Magdalen Hall.

Town
and
Gown

Visitors to Oxford, not to mention its student population, often seem to forget that the University is part of the City and not the other way around. Indigenous Oxonians get understandably frustrated and annoyed by this affront. Oxford was after all established as a Saxon settlement long before the academics took over. The irate young man in the following extract attempts to set the record straight.

"Always your University...riding rough-shod over us townspeople, taking away our liberties, lording it over us, treating us as though we were indeed only a city of lodging-house keepers with no history of our own."

"Now, have you shown these ladies the Castle and the Castle mound? have you shown them where stood Rewley Abbey, or even Osney, or where the chapel of St.

Bartholomew's Hospital still stands? I dare say you've taught them to look on the city wall as a mere picturesque adjunct to the gardens of New College and Merton, and to see in our Cathedral only the chapel of Christchurch. Haven't you now? – eh! now, hasn't he, ladies?'

We owned that we had not seen the Castle, nor the Castle mound, nor had we ever heard of Rewley Abbey; of St. Bartholomew's Hospital we were totally ignorant.

There and then our impetuous new friend haled us off to see something of the city. We followed him to the Castle …

… Bulwarks Alley, cried Mr Grant. Once this looked into the Castle Moat, where now there is a busy canal wharf; a quiet corner this, ladies, and visited by few. I could wish to end my days here in one of these grey cottages, forgotten by everyone, though so near the midst of everything … You can see here, ladies, something of the strong position of the old city, of the steep slope to the water, and you can see the great mound that was thrown up nearly a thousand years ago to protect the ford against the Danish pirates when they came harrying and burning on their way up the river. I shall have the memories of a thousand years to keep me company when I end my days in Bulwark Alley.

Our little gentleman looked away into the distance with eyes full of love for what he saw. "Don't you fancy that you can hear the sound of the Osney bells?" he said …

To the uninstructed the view was rather a sordid one; but to him, no doubt, knowing as he did what had been there, it was full of suggestion and charm. His fancy painted the Castle at our feet and the Abbey in the distance, so that he saw it all before him and heard the sound of Tom bell ringing in his early home...

A sharp turn beyond Paradise house brought us in sight of the immensely high wall of the Jail, which stands on part of the site of the Castle, and then we saw the splendid Norman tower of St. George, the only one that remains of the ring of towers which once guarded the Castle. Beneath it is the Castle Mill. Here for a space we were permitted to lean on the parapet, to watch the water running under the bridge, and to relish the perfect composition of the Norman tower, the high mill buildings, and the yellow carts being loaded with flour.

"And now to Osney, to all that is left of Osney Abbey."

We set off again across the railway and down a street of small houses until we came to the tall chimney of the electric station and to some farm-like buildings. Here there was an arched gateway of stone, the remains of a square-headed window, and fragments of stone mouldings, bases of columns, and pieces of window tracery lying at our feet.   "All that remains," said Mr. Grant, "of one of the noblest abbeys of England … It makes one mad to think of it … Come away! come away!' We went round by a mill-stream overhung by weeping willows, and crossed the lock-gates onto the towing-path. Beyond the river one looks away across the meadows to the low Cumnor Hills and to Wytham. This view must be much as it was when the monks of Osney had their home here and when Tom bell still rang out from Osney Tower. We went on along the tow path and saw more of the many winding streams that encircle Oxford. It would be blissful to spend long summer days in exploring them … We said 'Goodbye' at last on a bastion of the old wall …

"Well, ladies" said Mr. Grant, "I hope you are pleased, and that Oxford City will be more than a name only to you for the future." We thanked him many times and departed homewards.

ऒ

As those visitors discovered, the Castle and the remaining medieval houses are a reminder that the city has its own rich history, connected to but independent from the University. In the eighteenth century the Reverend Peshall, following in the footsteps of Anthony Wood, gives a detailed account of the Castle and describes an unfortunate event that took place there in the late sixteenth century.

The Chronicles of Oseney tell us, that it was began by Robert Doily, the first of that Name in England, Anno 1071, and finished by him 1073 … He raised it with digging deep Trenches to make the River run round it, and made high Hills wih lofty Towers and Walls theron, to overlook the town and Country adjacent; the Bilding of which cost but 20 Marks. The Vestigia of which though to the Beholder apparent to this day, yet the Glory and Splendor of the famous Edifices therein, as also those Fortifications adjoining are altogether diminished and buried in its own Rubbish. The Reason why this castle was built at this Time, was to quell and keep under the neighbouring Parts, especially the City of Oxford who, as i have said before, gave great Affronts and proved troublesome to King William in his thorough Conquest of this Country.

Which Castle, when built, proved good and convenient to the Conqueror; yet as it afterwards fell out, it was not only troublesome to the University by those frequent Skirmishes that there happened, but also in some Respect proved the Bane of his Children when they went together by the Ears for the Crown …

… A Remarkable Curiosity here is the Ruins of the ancient Town-Hall in the Castle-Yard, where in 1577 was held the Black Assizes, when the Lieutenant of the County, two Knights, eight Esquires and Justices of the peace, and almost all the Gentleman of the Grand Jury died quickly after their Return of the Poisonous smell of the Gaol, where the Prisoners had long been closely immured. Above one hundred Scholars, besides Townsmen, were seized with a Strange distemper, and ran about the streets like Madmen, and beat their Governors. This disaster lasted a Month.

හ

The relationship between Town and Gown has not always been entirely amicable. Townspeople have often resented the academic cuckoo that has taken over their nest, not to mention the centuries when the city was governed almost exclusively by the Chancellor of the University. Occasionally, the rivalry flared up into open hostilities on the streets of Oxford. It has even been claimed that more blood has been spilled on The High Street than on any battlefield in Europe! Thomas Hughes gives an account of a Town/Gown 'row' in Tom Brown at Oxford:

Five shopboys or scouts' boys, full of sauciness, loitering at an out-of-the-way street corner. Enter two freshmen, full of dignity and bad wine. Explosion of flammable material. Freshmen mobbed into High Street or Broad Street, where the tables are turned by the gathering of many more freshmen, and the mob of town boys quietly subsides, put its hands in its pockets, and ceases to shout "Town, town!" The triumphant freshmen march up and down for perhaps half an hour, shouting "Gown, gown," and looking furious, but not half sorry that the mob vanishes like mist at their approach. Then come the proctors, who hunt down, and break up the gown in some half-hour or hour. The 'town' again marches about in the ascendant, and mobs the scattered freshmen, wherever they can be caught, in very small numbers.

ങ

In previous centuries Town/Gown encounters were much more blood-thirsty. The most infamous battle occurred in the fourteenth century on the day of St. Scholastica, the virgin; February 10. Although lives were lost on both sides, the city of Oxford was blamed for the disturbance and for the next five hundred years the mayor and burgesses were made to pay a yearly fine and attend a penitential mass on the

anniversary of the battle. The quarrel all began over some
bad wine …

> To Swindlestock on Carfax
> A scholar young and gay
> With other scholars did repair
> To laugh the world away,
> Till, hot with wine, - "Ho, vintner,
> What trash is this we drink?"
> He cracked the quart-pot on his head
> And down John Vintner dropped for dead
> And his Blood ran black as ink, as ink,
> His blood ran black as ink.

> Raise the alarm, St. Mary's
> Here's danger for the Gown.
> "To arms! To arms!" St. Martin's
> Thunders across the Town.
> Then soft and slippered barbers
> Whip out their razors bright,
> And butchers whet the cleavers edge,
> And beggar folk from ditch and hedge
> Come thirsting for the fight, the fight,
> Ho! thirsting for the fight.

> From Inn and Hall and College
> With arrow and with bow
> Exultant press the scholars
> To battle blow for blow.

And Kibald Street is red with blood
And Beaumont fields are red,
And lively lads that rose this morn
Tonight besides St. Giles's bourne
Are lying stark and dead, aye, dead,
Are lying stark and dead.

The Chancellor to Woodstock
Has posted him in fear.
"God save your Majesty," he said
"Black are the doings here."
"'sblood!" cried the King, "Shall I not be
"Master in my own land?"
He ground the Town beneath his thumb.
"Down to the dungeon with the scum!"
And took the Chancellor's hand, smooth hand
And took the Chancellor's hand.

And year by year the Townsmen
Must go to church to pray
For blessed scholar-saints who died
Upon that bloody day.
And Gownsmen with a queasy mind
Must take the pence they pay,
While in St. Frideswide's cloister dim
A monk is at his evening hymn
Who once was young and gay, ah, gay,
Who once was young and gay.

St. Martin's Tower, the town's garrison during the Scholastica Day battle, stands at Carfax, or 'Fourways' as Hardy calls it, in the very centre of Oxford. With Cornmarket, The High Street, St. Aldates and Queen Street diverging like veins to the North, East, South and West, this crossroads has been the heart of the city from the earliest times:

The Beginning and Rise of the Said Streets are from Quatervois beforementioned, or the place which tendeth or looketh four Ways ... It was accounted the Meditullum of the City and the Heart of the Market, and the Chiefest Place where most sorts of Merchandise were exposed to Sale. The vulgar Name of it was Carfax, corrupted from Quatervois as some have thought, others will have it derived from Caerbos ie: the Caer or City of Boso, who was Consul of Oxford in King Arthur's Time. In the Middle of this Quadvirium or Fourways, a very fair and beautiful Conduit presents itself forth to us, such, for its Images of Ancient Kings about it, Gilding and exquisite Carving, the like is hardly to be found in England...

Formerly the Tower was much higher, and of a more stately Bulk, as also part of the Church; but by the command of King Edward III in the fourteenth year of his Reign, they were taken down lower, as now appears: Because upon the complaints of the Scholars, the Townsmen would, in Time of Combat with them, retire there as to their Castle, from thence gall and Annoy them with Arrows and Stones.

The Custom of ringing the Bell at Carfax every Night at

eight o'clock, (called Curfew Bell, or Cover-Fire-Bell) was by order of King Alfred, the Restorer of our University, who ordained that all the Inhabitants at Oxford should, at the ringing of that Bell, cover up their Fires and go to Bed, which Custom is observed to this day; and the Bell as constantly rings at Eight, as Great Tom tolls at Nine. It is also a Custom added to the former, after the ringing and tolling of this Bell, to let the inhabitants know the Day of the Month by so many Tolls.

At 'Fourways', Jude feels the pulse of Christminster life:

… that Crossway … had more history than the oldest college in the city. It was literally teeming, stratified, with the shades of human groups, who had met there for tragedy, comedy, farce; real enactments of the intensest kind. At Fourways men had stood and talked of Napoleon, the loss of America, the execution of King Charles, the burning of the Martyrs, the Crusades, the norman Conquest, possibly of the arrival of Caesar. Here the two sexes had met for loving, hating, coupling, parting; had waited, had suffered, for each other; had triumphed over each other; cursed each other in jealousy, blessed each other in forgiveness.

He began to see that the town life was a book of humanity infinitely more palpitating, varied and compendious than the gown life. These struggling men and women before him were the reality of Christminster, though they knew little of Christ or Minster. That was one of the humours of things. The floating population of students and teachers, who did know both in a way, were not Christminster in a local sense at all.

He looked at his watch, and, in pursuit of this idea, he went on till he came to a public hall, where a promenade concert was in progress. Jude entered, and found the room full of shop youths and girls, soldiers, apprentices, boys of eleven smoking cigarettes, and light women of the more respectable and amateur class. He had tapped the real Christminster life. A band was playing, and the crowd walked about and jostled each other, and every now and then a man got upon a platform and sang a comic song.

ᏣᎨ

The 'High' has claimed its share of admirers over the years. Wordsworth celebrated its 'stream-like windings' and even Mr Green Senior finds he can remember it from among the indistinct images he gathers in Oxford. Here is the Reverend Peshall again with his own description of Oxford's main thoroughfare.

The High-Street, 2038 feet long and 85 broad, is very neatly paved; and its sides adorned with the magnificent Colleges of Queens, University, and All Souls, the grand Churches of St. Mary and All Saints, with the embattled, decent Tower of Carfax at the extremity or End; and is not to be exceeded for Length, Beauty and Grandeur, anywhere; especially if we extend our view to the white Stone Bridge, of an elegant new Construction, over the River Cherwell, and on the lofty Tower and superb College of Magdalene. This Street owes much of its Beauty to its curve Direction, affording by this means a gradual and unexpected Display of its Parts, and successively surprises and pleases at every Turn with a new Object …

ℭ

Making up for its inferior length by its substantial breadth, Broad Street spreads out fatly from the corner of Cornmarket to the beginning of Parks Road, taking in Balliol and Trinity Colleges, the original University museum, the Sheldonian Theatre, and Blackwell's world-famous bookshop on the way. A cross in the road and a plaque on the wall of Balliol marks the spot where the Protestant bishops Hugh Latimer, Nicholas Ridley and Thomas Cranmer were burnt for their faith during the reign of Queen Mary. Latimer is supposed to have reassured his fellow sufferer with the following celebrated words:

"Be of good comfort, Master Ridley, and play the man. We shall this day light such a candle, by God's grace, in England, as I trust shall never be put out."

ℭ

Nathaniel Hawthorne was suitably moved by the bishops' story:

… the clock had sometime ago struck eleven, when we were passing under a long extent of antique wall and towers, which Durham said were those of Balliol College. He led us into

102

the middle of the street, and showed us a cross which was paved into it, on a level with the rest of the pavement. This was the spot where Latimer and Ridley, and another Bishop, were martyred in Bloody Mary's time. There is a memorial to them in another street; but this, where I set my foot at nearly midnight, was the very spot where their flesh turned to ashes, and their bones whitened.

But the incorrigible Zuleika Dobson is less easily affected:

The landau was rolling into 'the Broad', over that ground which had once blackened under the faggots lit for Latimer and Ridley. It rolled past the portals of Balliol and Trinity, past the Ashmolean. From those pedestals which intersperse the railings of the Sheldonian, the high grim busts of the Roman Emperors stared down at the fair stranger in the equipage. Zuleika returned their stare with but a casual glance. The inanimate had little charm for her.

୧

Max Beerbohm's novel, Zuleika Dobson, *is the epitome of Edwardian Oxford. During a visit to her grandfather, the heroine captures the hearts of the entire undergraduate population. They proceed to commit mass suicide in her honour by throwing themselves 'with single cries of 'Zuleika'!" into the Thames. The mock tragic progress of the novel is watched despairingly by the stone heads of the Emperors that surround the Sheldonian Theatre.*

Confusingly, the 'Theatre' is not the place to go if you want to see a good play; the Sheldonian was designed by the young Sir Christopher Wren as an arena for University ceremonies, Thomas Tickell (of course) loved it, and Daniel Defoe was also more than commonly impressed.

See where the sacred Sheldon's haughty Dome
Rivals the stately pomp of ancient Rome,

Whose Form so great and noble, seems design'd
T'express the Grandeur of its Founder's Mind.

Besides the Colleges, some of which are extremely fine and magnificent; there are some Publick Buildings which make a most glorious appearance: The first and greatest of all is the *Theatre*, a Building not to be equall'd by any thing of its kind in the World; no, not in *Italy* itself:

The Theatre at *Oxford* prepared for the publick Exercises of the Schools, and for the operations of the Learned Part of the *English* World only, is in its Grandeur and Magnificence, infinitely superior to any thing in the World of its Kind; it is a finish'd Peice as to its Building, the Front is exquisitely fine, the Columns and Pilasters regular, and very beautiful; 'tis all built of Free-stone: The Model was approv'd by the best Masters of Architecture at the time, in the Presence of K. *Charles II,* who was himself a very Curious Observer, and a good Judge; Sir *Christopher Wren* was the Director of the Work, as he was the person that drew the Model:

Archbishop *Sheldon*, they tell us, paid for it, and gave it to the University: There is a world of Decoration in the Front of it, and more beautiful Additions, by way of Ornament, besides the antient Inscription, than is to be seen any where in *Europe*; at least, where I have been.

ᙍ

The Sheldonian was also the original home of the Oxford University Press. In the seventeenth and eighteenth centuries curious visitors could have their names printed. To the uninitiated however, the goings-on were rather strange …

> Down in the cellar folks are doing
> Something that makes a world of bowing,
> Some throw Black-Balls, their Heads some throwing,
> As if they Arse-ward were a moving,
> Stooping a little more to view 'um,
> They kindly ask'd me to come to 'um,
>
> A world of Paper there was lying,
> Besides a deal as hung a drying,
> They being wet as I suppose,
> Were hung on Lines, as we hang Cloaths;
> The folk below began to hollow,
> Whop, you there, honest Country Fellow;
> We'll print your name, What is't I wonder?
> Says I, one's John (Sir), t'other's Blunder.

ᙍ

From the top of the Theatre, or the Spire of St Mary's, there is a magnificent birds-eye view of the beauties of the city and University:

My silent friend at the luncheon had told me that this is the way to see Oxford …

"When I have visitors" he said, "I take them up to the top of the theatre and I say, "There is Magdalen and there is Christchurch, there is New College and there the Bodleian Library. Here is half a crown. Go forth and see the sights and trouble me no more until evening." The man who can't amuse himself in Oxford must be a fool … we hardly knew where to turn first, for all the lovely city lay in the glowing sunshine at our feet.

Immediately beneath was the long narrow winding roof of the Bodleian Library; beyond this rose the swelling dome of the Camera Bodleiana; again beyond, the spire of the University Church with all its clustered pinnacles stood clear against the summer sky.

Faithfully with guide-book and with key-plan did we try to identitfy each tower and roof. Always beyond them stood the hills; on the east Headington Hill and Shotover rose behind the tower of New College; on the west the Berkshire Hills behind the slender fleche of Exeter College Chapel and the sturdy square towere of St. Michael's.

Looking northward we saw something of the newness and incongruity of modern Oxford. Much of it is mercifully hidden among bosky trees, but nothing could hide the terrible red and striped walls of Keble.

Likened, among other things, to a dinosaur wearing a Fair-isle sweater, Keble has always been frowned upon by the other colleges for the exuberance of its Victorian architecture. It seems to offer a red-brick rebuff to the mellow ancient stones of its elder sisters and a reminder that, even in Oxford, the middle ages cannot linger on for ever.

Beyond the dreaming spires

It may be Radcliffe Square which a tourist, eager for beauty and nostalgic for the past, remembers of Oxford, but the modern city extends far beyond this celebrated epicentre, stretching its twentieth century arms to embrace the former villages of Cowley, home of Morris Motors, Iffley, Headington and Botley, not to mention the wealthy North Oxford suburbs that grew up in the nineteenth century.

During the 1950s and '60s Maida Stanier, using the pseudonym 'Culex', wrote light verse for the Oxford Times. *Her 'Song of the Suburbs' describes the character of some of Oxford's outlying districts:*

෯

COWLEY

Up and down the Cowley Road,
In and out the Regal,
Betty Grable for the boys,
Me for Anna Neagle.

Bicycles five abreast on the road,
Prams three-deep on the pavement;
Mum's poshed up for the sales as if
She didn't know what to save meant.

Oxford Mail and slippers for Dad;
Tell those Planners to nark it.
Give us a Woolworth's of our own
And keep your old Cornmarket.

Fish and chips on Saturday night:
Football pools on Sunday:
(Auntie's won a new T.V.)
Back to work on Monday.

Cowley codgers never say die.
Hopes are what they're born in.
Bicycle shop tonight – who knows?
Lord Thingumijig in the morning!

So, up and down the Cowley Road,
In and out the Regal.
Betty Grable for the boys,
Me for Anna Neagle.

IFFLEY

Iffley is a private place
With a veil before her face.
You must grow with her in grace
If you would know Iffley.

School and barn and almshouse gray
Line the drowsy street: in May
Chestnut candles burn all day
By the church at Iffley.

Green and gold the meadows blow.
Gypsies and the children know
Where the fritillaries grow
In the fields at Iffley.

On the circumambient streams
Floats the swan in summer dreams,
And the lonely heron schemes
In the reeds at Iffley.

"Easy all," the coxes cry
At the weir: and in reply
"Easy all," the ghosts and I
Whisper down at Iffley.

HEADINGTON HILL

Headington Hill, Headington Hill,
They're stout of lung and steady of will
Who live at the top of Headington Hill,
Superior folks, who prefer a view,
Not river bound like me and you.
Their streets have a whim of dropping away
Over expanses wild and gray,
– You'd swear the sea will be there some day –
And the winds they breathe come strong and pure,
Bucketing over bleak Otmoor
To Shotover-side where secret roads
Are pointed to Whipsnade-like abodes
By sinister signposts. (Did you see
A wolf go loping behind that tree?)
Yes, civilisation's pretty thin
On Headington Hill. But they won't give in.
Though every morning sucks them down
A dappled tunnel towards the town,
Evening washes them back again,
Riding the breakers over the 'Plain'
Up the tunnel and out, until
They're safely home on Headington Hill.

McGONIGAL ON BOTLEY

Ah, Botley!
I adore thee hotly,
(And I shall shortly disclose the reason why),
Even though you've a raddled
Look, as if saddled
With the need to keep up appearances or die.

You have a canal,
Rather blank and banal,
And a river for swans and for tiddlers a brook.

And the toffs up at Cumnor
Make the Botley Road hum, nor
Give their surroundings so much as a look.

BUT THEY'RE WRONG
As I'll prove in my song.
In one respect Botley is entirely unique.
Beneficicent Botley,
I adore thee hotly
For the divine afflatus of marmalade, balm to my
                              soul, twice a week.

⋈

Botley, the area of West Oxford beyond the station, is the home of the famous Oxford marmalade, which began its career in Frank Cooper's shop on the High Street in the nineteenth century.

NORTH OXFORD

It is one thing to write poems
About Iffley, Headington or even Cowley,
But North Oxford is another matter.
North Oxford is quite capable of writing its own poems,
Setting them to music and staging them in pageants.
North Oxford is highbrow.
Its housewives are lean and angry
From rushing up and down so many basement stairs,
And its fathers are breathless
From bicycling madly to Nursery School
On their way to the Lab.
The houses run to amiable eccentricities
Like turrets,
And the gardens are better at trees than flowers,
Which may, or may not explain
Why there is such a thin sprouting of television aerials.
A last infirmary, one might say, of noble minds,
But not
A place about which to write a poem.

03

In recent years North Oxford has also become home to another great fictional figure. In 'a nondescript block of flats at the top of the Banbury Road' lives the enigmatic and irascible Inspector Morse, Chief Inspector of the Thames Valley Police. Morse's investigations take him to all parts of the city including the area, bizarrely and inexplicably known as Jericho, that backs onto the canal, to the north-west of St. Giles' and the Woodstock Road.

Here, imperceptibly at first, but soon quite unmistakeably, the University has been left behind, and even the the vast building on the left which houses the Oxford University Press, its lawned quadrangle glimpsed through the high wrought-iron gates, looks bleakly out of place and rather lonely, like some dowager duchess at a discotheque...

... But the visitor to the City Museum in St Aldates will find no *Guide to Jericho* along the shelves; and even by the oldest of its own inhabitants, the provenance of that charming and mysterious name of 'Jericho' is variously – and dubiously – traced. Some claim that in the early days the whistle of a passing train from the lines across the canal could make the walls come tumbling down; others would point darkly to the synagogue in Richmond Road and talk of sharp and profitable dealings in the former Jewish quarter; yet others lift their eyes to read the legend on a local inn: 'Tarry ye at Jericho until your beards be grown'. But the majority of the area's inhabitants would just look blankly at their interlocutors, as if they had been asked such obviously unanswerable questions as why it was that men were born, or why they should live or die, and fall in love with booze or women.

ଔ

Nathaniel Hawthorne was fortunate enough to stay in a house in St. Giles when he visited Oxford.

I have seen few pleasanter scenes than this street in which we lodge, with its spacious breadth, its two rows of fine old trees, with side-walks as wide as the whole width of ordinary streets, and, on the opposite side, the rows of houses, some of them ancient with picturesque gables, partially disclosed through the intervening foliage … From our window, we have a slantwise glimpse to the right of the walls of St. John's College; and the general aspect of the street is of an antiquity not to shame those medieval halls. Our own lodgings are in a house that seems to be very old, with panelled walls, beams across the ceiling [sic], lattice windows in the chambers, and a musty fragrance, such as old houses inevitably have.

ଔ

Named after the church at its northern end, this long, elegant tree-lined street is transformed for two days in early September. During the St. Giles' Fair, the din of the traffic is replaced by the clanking of fairground machinery, the beeping of horns by the shrieks of the fairgoers and the smell of fumes by the hot, sweetly acrid aroma of candy-floss, toffee apples, hamburgers and chips. The facades of Balliol and St. John's look on in discomfort at the sight of the town enjoying itself, as the fair brazenly illuminates their august windows with flashing fluorescent lights.

St. Giles is also home to one of Oxford's well-known pubs; The Eagle and Child or Bird and Baby as it was affectionately called by some of its most famous drinkers. C.S. Lewis, his brother William Lewis, J.R.R. Tolkien and Christopher Williams, otherwise known as the Inklings, used to meet here to discuss the books they were working on. The pub crops up several times in the letters of J.R.R. Tolkien.

'I know no more pleasant sound than arriving at the 'B and B' and hearing a roar, and knowing that one can plunge in."

(to C.S. Lewis)

'This morning I lectured, and found the Bird and Baby closed; but was hailed in a voice that carried across the torrent of vehicles that was once St. Giles, and discovered the two Lewises and C.Williams, high and very dry on the other side. Eventually we got four pints of passable ale at the 'King's Arms' - at a cost of 5/8 ... I hope to see the lads tomorrow; otherwise life is as bright as water in a ditch ... '

(to C. Tolkien)

I wonder what Tolkien would make of the traffic problems that beset St. Giles nowadays, not to mention the price of beer in the King's Arms ...

If the hub-bub of modern Oxford becomes too much, and you have had all you can take of the grandeur of the University buildings, it is still possible to step back in time, through the narrow lanes and passages off Holywell Street, as the writer does in Oxford From Within:

… he turned to the right up Holywell by the little aged odd-shaped houses of stucco and stone and old-red brick, on which the new buildings of New College whitely stare. The hall-doors, sometimes of old oak, touch the pavement; to some there is a step down from the pavement, some you must surely stoop to enter, unless you are very small of stature. There is every shape of window, but most are latticed. As you walk along, some windows are on a level with your waist, and then you glance down to catch a glimpse through green curtains of wonderful interiors, where great brown beams cross the ceilings, where there are strange old grates and fire-places, where the ceilings slope and the floors quaintly undulate. Our friend seemed to be in another world to that in which the commodious villas flourished. In these old houses exciting people must have lived, they were the homes of scholars, antiquaries, poets: those commodious villas merely told comfortable stories of comfort … The old houses were built for people to live in; …

But our friend turned down Bath Place, and got even further from the modern world of newspapers and villas. Bath Place is an alley for footmen, which zig-zags by tiny houses and rambling little cottages, and eventually comes out (if you have not previously lost yourself) in New College Street, which becomes Queen's Lane, in the same way as Fleet Street becomes the Strand. If you get as far as the bewildering middle of Bath Place and in finding the right way under the arch between two houses have not penetrated so many private abodes that you shamefacedly turn back before the way becomes normally clear, then look round to the left and you will see above a tree and a wall a tower of New College most darkly and most beautifully rising into the sky. For just where the maze becomes easy, and you may after much stooping and crampedness straighten out your mind and body, the prospect widens to a surprising change. The tiny rambling houses cluster round high dark walls and the high dark tower rises superbly from its clustered surroundings. You seem to see it then as you were meant to see it.

❧

Accompanied by a variety of famous and obscure characters, this anthology of Oxford has taken us around the city and University down famous streets and into celebrated colleges. Throughout its pages, we have charted the attempts of poets and essayists, novelists and playwrights to express the essence of Oxford in language both exalted and comical. Their web of words creates a literary Oxford, that merges and blends into the stones and streets of the physical city:

Beautiful city! So venerable, so lovely, so unravaged by the fierce intellectual life of our century, so severe! 'There are our young barbarians all at play!' And yet, steeped in sentiment as she lies, spreading her gardens to the moonlight, and whispering from her towers the last enchantments of the Middle Age, who will deny that Oxford, by her ineffable charm, keeps ever calling us nearer to the true goal of all of us, to the ideal, to perfection, – to beauty in a word, which is only truth seen from another side ... Adorable dreamer, whose heart has been so romantic! who hast given thyself so prodigally, given thyself to sides and heroes not mine, only never to the Philistines! home of lost causes, and forsaken beliefs, and unpopular names, and impossible loyalties!

(Matthew Arnold: *Essays in Criticism*, 1865)

 G3

And finally, my Oxford:

A place of intoxicating beauty and maddening prejudices;
Of books and boats and yellow light;
Of intense self-obsession and glorious self-parody;
Bicycles, buses, and pure delight.

G3

Sources and Acknowledgements ~

The compiler wishes to express her gratitude to the staff of both the Bodleian Library and The Centre for Oxfordshire Studies, and to Marjorie Szurko of Keble College Library, for affording research facilities; and to the copyright owners individually acknowledged below for permitting quotation from copyright material.

9: Thomas Tickell, *Oxford, a Poem*, 1707.

10: Ralph Aga, *Map of Oxford*, 1578.

10-1: Celia Fiennes, *The Journeys of ...* (ed. John Hillaby), 1983.

11-2: Daniel Defoe, *Tour thro' the whole Island of Great Britain, vol.1*, 1724.

12-3: Hugh de Selincourt, *Oxford From Within*, 1910.

14-5: Anthony Wood, *History and Antiquities of the City of Oxford*, ed. Andrew Clarke, 1889.

15-6: Gascoigne Mackie, 'Charmides' in *The Glamour of Oxford*, ed. William Knight, 1911.

16: Matthew Arnold, *The Oxford Poems of ...*, 1910 ('Thyrsis', 1866).

17: Thomas Hardy, *Jude the Obscure*, 1895, Papermac edition (reproduced by permission of Macmillan General Books).

17-8: Rev. Edward Bradley, *The Adventures of Mr. Verdant Green*, 1853.

18-9: C.S. Lewis, *The Letters of ...*, 1966 (reproduced by permission of Harper Collins).

19-20: John Keats, *The Letters of ...*, ed. M.B. Forman, 4th ed. 1952.

20-1: Gerard Manley Hopkins, *The Poems of ...*, ed. by W.H. Gardner and N.H. Mackensie, 4th ed. 1967.

21: Thomas Tickell, *Oxford, a Poem*, 1707.

21: Thomas Warton, *The Triumph of Isis*, 1749.

22-3: Nathaniel Hawthorne, *The English Notebooks*, 1884, ed. Randall Stewart,1941.

24-5: Rev. Edward Bradley, *The Adventures of Mr. Verdant Green*, 1853.

25-6: Maida Stanier, *Culex's Guide to Oxford*, 1955.

27-8: Thomas Hardy, *Jude the Obscure*, 1895, Papermac edition (reproduced by permission of Macmillan General Books).

28-9: Oona Howard Ball, *Barbara Goes to Oxford*, 1907.

31: John Keats, *The Letters of ...*, ed. M.B. Forman, 4th ed. 1952.

32: John Taylor, *The Water Poet*, 1632.

32-3: Edmund Spenser, *The Faerie Queene, Book IV*, 1596.

34-5: Thomas Hughes, *Tom Brown at Oxford*, 1886.

35-6: Rev. Edward Bradley, *The Adventures of Mr. Verdant Green*, 1853.

37-9: Rhoda Broughton, *Belinda*, 1883.

39-40: C.L. Dodgson (Lewis Carroll), *Alice in Wonderland*, 1865.

40: John Ross, *Historia Regium Angliae*, 1468, in Rev. Sir J. Peshall, *The Antient and Present State of the City of Oxford*, 1773.

41: Thomas Warton, *The Companion to the Guide*, 1760.

41-2: Anthony Wood, *History and Antiquities of the City of Oxford*, ed. Andrew Clarke, 1889.

42-3: *ibid.*

45-6: William Harrison, *Description of England*.

46: Anon., *A Week in Oxford*, 1817.

47: George Colman, *An Oxonian in Town*, 1769.

48: Thomas Hardy, *Jude the Obscure*, 1895, Papermac edition (reproduced by permission of Macmillan General Books).

48-9: Nathaniel Hawthorne, *The English Notebooks*, 1884, ed. Randall Stewart, 1941.

49-50: Celia Fiennes, *The Journeys of ...* (ed. John Hillaby), 1983.

50-2: C.S. Lewis, *The Letters of ...*, 1966 (reproduced by permission of Harper Collins)

52-3: Anon., *A Week in Oxford*, 1817.

53: Oona Howard Ball, *Barbara Goes to Oxford*, 1907.

54-5: Maida Stanier, *Culex Rides Again*, 1976.

56: Thomas Churchyard (1520-1604), *The Tragedy of Cardinal Wolsey* (published with George Cavendish, *The Life of Cardinal Wolsey*, 1885).

56-7: Bishop Richard Corbet (1582-1635), *Great Tom*.

57-8: Joseph Henry Shorthouse, *John Inglesant*, 1902.

59: Karl Baedeker, *Guide to Great Britain*, 1887.

59-60: William Harrison, *Description of England*.

60-1: Anthony Wood, *History and Antiquities of the City of Oxford*, ed. Andrew Clarke, 1889.

61-2: Robert Greene, *Frier Bacon and Frier Bongay*, 1594.

62-3: William Cobbett, *Rural Rides*, 1830.

63: Sir Humphrey Prideaux, *Letters to John Ellis 1674-1722*, ed. E.M. Thompson, 1875.

63-4: Edward Gibbon, *Miscellaneous Works with Memoirs of my Life*, 1796.

64-5: Hugh de Selincourt, *Oxford From Within*, 1910.

67-8: Daniel Defoe, *Tour thro' the whole Island of Great Britain, vol.1*, 1724.

68-9: Henry Vaughan, *The Pass-times and Diversions of a Countrey Muse*, 1678.

68: John Owen, *Epigrams*, 1612.

69: Chiang Lee, *The Silent Traveller*, 2nd. ed. 1945.

69: Robert Burton, *The Anatomy of Melancholy*, 1605.

70: Oona Howard Ball, *Barbara Goes to Oxford*, 1907.

70-1: Count Lorenzo Magolotti, *The Travels of Cosimo III*, 1821.

71-2: Alicia D'anvers, *Academia*, 1691.

72-4: C.S. Lewis, *The Letters of …*, 1966 (reproduced by permission of Harper Collins).

74: Thomas Hughes, *Tom Brown at Oxford*, 1886.

77-8: Jane Austen, *Northanger Abbey*, 1818.

78-9: Geoffrey Chaucer, *Canterbury Tales*, c. 1390.

79-80: Alicia D'anvers, *Academia*, 1691.

80-1: Nicholas Amherst, *Strephon's Revenge*, 1718.

81-2: Thomas Warton, *The Oxford Sausage*, 1764.

82: Nathaniel Hawthorne, *The English Notebooks*, 1884, ed. Randall Stewart,1941.

83-4: Evelyn Waugh, *Brideshead Revisited*, 1945.

84-6: Oona Howard Ball, *Barbara Goes to Oxford*, 1907.

86-7: Renée Haynes, *Neapolitan Ice*, 1928.

87: C.S. Lewis, *The Letters of …*, 1966 (reproduced by permission of Harper Collins).

88: Edward Gibbon, *Miscellaneous Works with Memoirs of my Life*, 1796.

89: Anthony Wood, *Modus Salium*.

91-4: Oona Howard Ball, *Barbara Goes to Oxford*, 1907.

94-5: Rev. Sir J. Peshall, *The Antient and Present State of the City of Oxford*, 1773.

96: Thomas Hughes, *Tom Brown at Oxford*, 1886.

97-9: Maida Stanier, *Culex's Guide to Oxford*, 1955.

99-100: Rev. Sir J. Peshall, *The Antient and Present State of the City of Oxford*, 1773.

100-1: Thomas Hardy, *Jude the Obscure*, 1895, Papermac edition (reproduced by permission of Macmillan General Books)

101-2: Rev. Sir J. Peshall, *The Antient and Present State of the City of Oxford*, 1773.

103: Sir Max Beerbohm, *Zuleika Dobson*, 1911 (reproduced by permission of Reed Books).

104: Thomas Tickell, *Oxford, a Poem*, 1707.

104-5: Daniel Defoe, *Tour thro' the whole Island of Great Britain, vol.1*, 1724.

105: Alicia D'anvers, *Academia*, 1691.

106: Oona Howard Ball, *Barbara Goes to Oxford*, 1907.

110-4: Maida Stanier, *Culex's Guide to Oxford*, 1955.

115-6: Colin Dexter, *The Dead of Jericho*.

116: Nathaniel Hawthorne, *The English Notebooks*, 1884, ed. Randall Stewart,1941.

117: J.R.R. Tolkien, *The Letters of …*, ed. H. Carpenter with C. Tolkien (reproduced by permission of Harper Collins)

118-9: Hugh de Selincourt, *Oxford from Within*, 1910.

120: Matthew Arnold, *Essays in Criticism*, 1865.

Alma Mater: (Latin: beauteous mother) name given to any University, school, etc. by affectionate students.

Ashmolean: Museum opened in 1638 and named after its patron, the antiquarian Elias Ashmole. Originally located in a building next to the Bodleian Library in Broad Street, the museum now dominates Beaumont Street.

Binsey: village to the north west of Oxford.

blade: technical term for an oar.

Bloody Mary: Mary I (1516-1558). Daughter of Henry VIII and Catholic monarch of England from 1553. She was known as Bloody Mary because of the number of Protestants executed during her reign.

Chancellor: honorific head of Oxford University.

to catch a crab: rowing term, meaning to sink the blade incorrectly so that the rower is forced sharply backwards in the boat.

to come up: to take up residence at the University.

Dean: college official in charge of discipline.

Don: University teacher, from the Latin 'dominus'.

feather: rowing term, meaning to turn the blade so that it is parallel with the surface of the water when it is not submerged.

fellow: member of a college.

Gown: the University (as opposed to 'Town'). A reference to academic dress.

Gownsman: a student

The Gut: particularly narrow part of the river Thames below Christ Church meadows.

kine: cows, from the Old English *cy*.

Law, Locke and Newton: William Law (1686-1761) English churchman and writer, educated at Emmanuel College, Cambridge. **John Locke** (1632-1704) English philosopher, author of the *Essay concerning Human Understanding* (1690), educated at Christ Church, Oxford.

to matriculate: to be enrolled at a college, from Latin *matricula*, rolls.

Maudlin: early spelling of Magdalen. The pronunciation has remained the same.

Mitre or Tuns: Oxford ale-houses.

Modius Salium: A peck of salt (approx.).

The Other Place: Cambridge.

Sir Isaac Newton (1642-1727) English scientist and mathematician, educated at Trinity College, Cambridge.

O.U.D.S.: Oxford University Dramatic Society, pronounced 'Owds'.

passman: student who gets a 'pass' as opposed to an 'Honours' degree.

to plough: to fail an examination.

to pluck: to fail another examination.

proctor: University officer responsible for discipline. First mentioned in the thirteenth century.

punt: a flat-bottomed boat propelleled by means of a long pole being pushed against the river-bed.

Schools: abbrev. of Examination Schools; both the building and the Final examinations that take place inside it

sculling: solo rowing.

tope: to drink hard regularly.

trencher: the mortarboard or University hat.

tub: supposedly stable and unsinkable boat shaped like a tub.

The Union: University club, and debating society.

Woodstock: village to the north of Oxford. Location of Blenheim Palace.

Subject Index ~

Author Index ~

Sophie Blacksell read English and German at Keble College, graduating in the summer of 1996. After a brief period of post-Finals recuperation she once more buried herself in the libraries of Oxford to unearth the intriguing treasures which make up this affectionate selection.